MW01707591

CRIMINAL ACTS 2

CRIMINAL ACTS 2

The Canadian True Crime Annual

Lee Lamothe

Macmillan Canada
Toronto

Canadian Cataloguing in Publication Data

Criminal acts : the Canadian true crime annual

Annual.

[No.] 1 (1994)–

ISSN 1198-5925

ISBN 0-7715-7369-3 (2nd issue)

HV6807.C74 364.1'5'097105 C95–300305–1 rev

Macmillan Canada wishes to thank the Canada Council, the Ontario Arts Council and the Ontario Ministry of Culture and Communications for supporting its publishing program.

Cover Design: Sharon Matthews

Cover Photo: Derek Ruttan/Canada Wide

Composition: IBEX Graphic Communications Inc.

Macmillan Canada
A Division of Canada Publishing Corporation
Toronto, Canada

1 2 3 4 5 99 98 97 96 95

Printed in Canada

For Lucy K. White, Michelle and Katie

CONTENTS

ACKNOWLEDGMENTS

THE SAYING GOES: Old friends are good, but new friends aren't too bad either.

Putting together *Criminal Acts 2*, I leaned heavily on a network of old friends, making many visits to the Favor Bank. (The Favor Bank is what makes much of the world run: a good deed done for you today is like a loan that can be called in anytime. This was a good arrangement at the beginning of the book when I had ten years' worth of daily reporting favors to collect; at the end the balance of trade leans heavily against me.) A lot of people got a lot of calls at all hours of the day and night. Faxes flew into Toronto from east and west. My contact book is thick with new home phone numbers, office numbers, pagers, cell phones, bars and even a yoga clinic.

In short, there are a lot of people to thank.

The usual suspects. Among them: Scot Magnish of the *Toronto Sun*; Maggie Whitcroft of CTV; Robert Benzie of the *Toronto Sun*; Sue Sgambati of Global Television, Peter Edwards of the *Toronto Star*, James Wallace of the *Toronto Sun*, Antonio Nicaso of the *Corriere Canadese*, Betsy Powell of Canadian Press, Stuart Hunter of the *Vancouver Province*, Lucy White of the *Financial Post*, and RCMP Supt. Wayne Blackburn and Det.-Sgt. Jim Crowley of the Metropolitan Toronto Police Homicide Squad.

The "new friends" include Alan Hustak of the Montreal *Gazette*, John Valorzi, Atlantic bureau chief for Canadian Press, Warren Goulding of the *Saskatoon Star Phoenix*, Don Curren of the *Regina Leader Post*, Mike D'Amour of the *Winnipeg Sun*, Rob Roberts of the *Halifax Daily News*, and Pete Vermeltfoort of the *Financial Post*.

And, nameless because of space constraints, are the dozens of reporters who filed the stories I relied heavily upon. Their coverage was without exception clearly researched and concisely written. If Canada has world-class crime, it also has world-class reporters to cover it.

Finally, to Allan Gould, who wrote *Criminal Acts 1* in 1994: the gratitude a traveller feels for the mapmaker.

INTRODUCTION

FITTING A YEAR of crime in Canada into a single book is like fitting a tall, fat corpse into a short, narrow coffin: you can do it, but when you're finished you don't end up with quite what you started out with. You fold and bend, and cut a little here and trim a little there. Then you sit on the lid to keep the casket closed down while you fasten the hasps.

Putting *Criminal Acts 2* together, I found crime isn't just about good guys and bad guys. The 1994 murder of Toronto police constable Todd Baylis wasn't just a cops-and-robbers tragedy. The topics of race and immigration moved front and center very quickly when it was determined that the accused shooter in the case was black and in Canada illegally, the immigration department having failed to deport him to Jamaica. The Metropolitan Toronto Police Association has sued the federal government over their handling of the accused man's case. There were renewed calls for capital punishment. The case was further complicated in March after a lengthy investigation by the force's internal affairs unit. Four of Baylis's brother officers, some of them the first to arrive at the scene of the Baylis shooting, were charged after allegations that drugs were planted on suspects.

Across Canada attacks on women—often sex-related murders—have moved beyond the tragic. Victims' rights groups are enraged that many of the accused men are on parole, usually from sentences involving similar incidents. Instead of asking the sad rhetorical "Why?" people are asking a very angry "Why, damn it?" Rights groups are demanding changes to the justice and penal systems, and victims and their families are making powerful impact statements to the courts before the convicted assailants are sentenced.

There are issues that go beyond the Criminal Code. Should communities reject attempts to have convicted child molesters released in their communities, even after the men have completed their sentences? Should a judge ban publication of a trial's proceedings, as one did in the Karla Homolka case? Is drunkenness a legitimate criminal defense? Is mercy killing any different than any killing? Do we want to pay for community-based policing? Should criminal profits be returned to the police to offset the cost of investigations? Should there be a fixed, lengthy sentence for using a handgun during the commission of a crime? All are questions that affect a broader public policy than simple policing and justice.

During 1994 there were several organized crime probes under way. Many are still going on; some may not end until 1996 because of the complexity of the investigations. Chasing the various mafias operating in Canada—and there are several—is no longer a case of traditional policing. Specialized financial cases involving foreign governments, particularly in the former Soviet Union, have taxed the resources of police forces across Canada whose members are well trained in crime fighting but less so in the intricacies of international finance.

Outlaw motorcycle gangs across Canada are locked in fierce struggles to control vice crimes, particularly in Quebec and southern Ontario. While Colombian cocaine cartel networks are quietly continuing their sophisticated trade in major urban centers, strict enforcement is driving them into smaller cities across the West and in the Maritimes. Gangsters from the former Soviet Union—many of them ex-KGB agents and professional criminals—are using Canada as a massive money laundry. East African and Asian crime syndicates are busily operating fraud, counterfeiting and drug trafficking operations across Canada.

The face of organized crime changes as new lines of influence are cut in the underworld territories.

Many people are lulled by the lack of overt violence in the underworld across the country. But rather than indicating a lack of activity, a quiet underworld indicates that everyone is busily working away.

Many foreign police forces are working with the RCMP, CSIS and other specialized intelligence organizations as Canadian criminals and Canada-related probes continue overseas.

Three police operations against organized crime were completed during the writing of this book. All are examples of the innovative types of investigations that go beyond reactive policing. In each case the police forces involved carried the fight to the targeted individuals.

For ten years I covered crime as a daily newspaper reporter in Toronto. The tendency of anyone working a crime beat in Toronto (or Vancouver or Montreal, for that matter) is to believe he or she is operating at the center of the universe. But while researching *Criminal Acts 2,* I quickly came to understand that crime isn't just a phenomenon in the Big Three urban centers. Across the country I found violence and brutality that rivaled any stories set in Toronto. The death of John Ryan Turner on the East Coast and the killing of Melanie Carpenter on the West had just as powerful an affect on their communities as the Bernardo–Homolka case had on southern Ontario. It became very clear to me that there's a trend, whether new or just newly discovered, in Canada to a lessening value of human life, that there's a depravity growing anywhere people live together.

And it was surprising how much crime there is. Early in the research I was overwhelmed by the sheer volume of stories. This brought about the problem of what to leave in and what to leave out. How much space would go to each incident? Whose murder got the most prominence?

There are no short stories when it comes to violent crime. No one should be killed and have their life and death relegated to eight column inches. In ten years, covering hundreds of homicides and violent crimes, I can't think of one I couldn't have gone a little further on, that I didn't feel deserved just a little more work, a little more care or a little more time.

In the late 1980s a woman's body was found on a Saturday afternoon in a yuppie part of Toronto where a lot of media people lived. Two of us went out and covered the story. The woman was found in a parkette, her pants pulled halfway down her thighs. She'd recently had sexual intercourse. It was a front-page story on Sunday morning, but later that day it turned out she was a boozehound from a midtown welfare rooming house. On Monday morning her story was buried in the middle of the paper.

Whether we have ten percent of the number of homicides of the United States, or a tenth of the serial killers, has little bearing on how we measure ourselves. Saying we're not as bad as the United States is meaningless: we should compare ourselves with ourselves, with our own past and our own values. If the statistics show we're less likely this year than last to be victims of crime, we have no reason to feel complacent. If the statistics show we're less afraid to walk the streets at night, this doesn't mean we're safer. Any homicide detective knows that if the murder rate falls off in any year, it doesn't necessarily mean we're less bloodthirsty. It probably means the paramedics and trauma centers are more efficient. Or the current crop of people who find homicide in their hearts are perhaps lacking the skills to be as thorough as they meant to be.

Having pointed out the flaws in our perception and how much or little attention a crime gets, I have to admit I, too, am a violator. The stories in this book are not as complete as they could or should be. Some cases should by themselves be entire books. The amount of space given isn't a yardstick of their value. Many cases were left out; this was due solely to space limitations.

The stories will be presented simply as what they are: glimpses at the trends that make up crime in Canada.

THE TRIAL OF PAUL BERNARDO

FOR ALMOST TWO years, the secrecy surrounding the Paul Bernardo murder case sparked gruesome speculation about the details of the killings of school girls Kristen French and Leslie Mahaffy.

But the reality that began to unfold in courtroom 6–1 when the trial opened in Toronto on May 18, 1995 was even more horrific than anyone imagined.

Crown prosecutor Ray Houlahan, speaking almost in a monotone, told the hushed courtroom a graphic tale of kidnapping and sexual slavery; of murder and rape and depravity.

Houlahan said Paul Bernardo and Karla Homolka had videotaped much of their sex crime spree; he also said the videotapes would be shown to the jury.

Karla Homolka, who had already pleaded guilty to manslaughter, was serving a twelve-year prison sentence as part of a secret plea bargain arrangement. Houlahan revealed that she would testify against her ex-husband Bernardo and presented her to the jury as a victim of the beastly Bernardo; an abused woman who was beaten and blackmailed into participating in the sexual assault and murders of Mahaffy and French.

In the fall of 1987, when the couple met, Paul Bernardo was twenty-three-years old. Tall and blond, he had graduated from the University of Toronto, where he'd studied business. He dressed well, dated numerous women, and dreamed of being both wealthy and famous. His high school year book described Bernardo as "Stud." He lived with his parents in a quiet neighborhood in Scarborough, a suburb of Toronto.

Seventeen-year-old Karla Homolka was attending a pet convention in a Scarborough hotel when she met Bernardo. Just over five-feet tall, Karla was a blue-eyed blonde, attractive and outgoing. She loved animals—in biology class she wouldn't participate in dissections—and was working part-time at a pet shop near her school in St. Catharines, west of Toronto.

The couple hit it off from the beginning. Within hours of meeting they were in Karla's hotel room engaging in a night of sex. As the relationship grew, Bernardo commuted back and forth to St. Catharines. Her parents solved the distance problem by letting Bernardo stay over on weekends. He became like a son to them.

During Christmas, 1989, Bernardo and Karla became engaged, appearing to friends and family as a pair of attractive, well-matched suburban yuppies. But behind the facade of normalcy, a deadly chemistry was at work—a mixture of murder and sexual lust that would leave three young women dead.

THE PROSECUTION

Houlahan's opening statement set forth, in broad strokes, the prosecution's case against Paul Bernardo:

On Christmas Eve, 1990 Karla Homolka, with the aid of halothane she stole from her employer's clinic, helped Bernardo drug her younger sister, Tammy. (Bernardo, who had by this time moved in with the Homolkas, had a yen for the 15-year-old blond Tammy.) A session of sexual abuse began, with Karla and Bernardo assaulting the unconscious girl by turns. It was all captured on videotape. By the end of the assault, Tammy had died, apparently choking on her own vomit—her death was tentatively ruled accidental. After her sister's funeral, Karla took up residence with Bernardo in a rented house on Bayview Drive, in Port Dalhousie.

The following year, on one June night while out prowling, Bernardo stumbled upon Leslie Mahaffy locked out of her home. Abducted from her own backyard and driven to the Bayview Drive home, the blindfolded fourteen-year-old underwent twenty-four hours of sexual abuse by Karla and Bernardo. Fearing the blindfold had slipped, and that she could identify him, Bernardo allegedly strangled Leslie with a length of electrical cord and left her body in their basement. That night, the couple prepared a Father's Day dinner for Karla's parents. Sometime the next day Leslie's body was cut into ten pieces—with the use of a circular saw—encased in cement, and dumped into nearby Lake Gibson.

Twelve days later, on June 29, 1991, Karla and Bernardo were married. On that same day, police divers were recovering Leslie Mahaffy's body parts from Lake Gibson.

Soon after their honeymoon in Hawaii, a young friend of the couple's was invited to the Bayview Drive home, drugged unconscious and sexually assaulted. Again, the incident was videotaped.

The following spring, on April 16, 1992, Kristen French was abducted from a church parking lot. Karla, luring the fifteen-year-old to the couple's car on the pretense that she needed directions, helped Bernardo kidnap the teen. Kristen, too, was taken to the Bayview Drive home where she underwent three days of sexual abuse by the couple. The attacks on Kristen were also videotaped. On April 19, because Karla and Bernardo were to attend Easter dinner at the Homolkas', Kristen was strangled to death, allegedly with the same electrical cord that was used on Leslie Mahaffy. That night, after dinner, the couple dumped Kristen's body in a ditch north of Burlington.

In January 1993, Karla left Bernardo claiming she'd been badly beaten with a flashlight. She entered extensive negotiations with police, eventually making several statements about the Mahaffy–French murders. On February 17, Bernardo was arrested and charged with two counts each of first-degree murder, kidnapping, forcible confinement, aggravated sexual assault, and one count of doing an indignity to a human body. A lengthy, detailed search of the Bayview Drive home was carried out and police seized several pieces of evidence. (The videotapes, however, wouldn't be discovered for some time after that.)

In July, Karla pleaded guilty to two counts of manslaughter and was sentenced to twelve years in prison—with the possibility of parole in 1997. The court ordered that details of the case and her deal with the government remain secret until Bernardo's murder trial.

Seven months later, the couple were divorced.

In September 1994 Bernardo's lawyer, Ken Murray, asked to be taken off the case. He turned over to police six incriminating videotapes that had come into his possession.

Amidst a swirl of horrific rumor and outrage at the relatively light sentence handed Karla Homolka, a restless public and press waited for the Bernardo trial to begin, for the videos to be shown, and for Homolka to get into the witness box.

In contrast to the notorious, at times tedious, and ongoing O.J. Simpson trial in Los Angeles—a hearing bogged down by the splitting of legal hairs and rounds of infighting among lawyers—the Bernardo trial got off to a swift start and maintained its momentum throughout the summer.

With the selection of John Rosen, it was generally agreed Bernardo couldn't have made a better choice from the pool of criminal lawyers in Toronto. Rosen, a tough cross-examiner who had defended more than 100 murder suspects, was backed by Tony Bryant, an aggressive lawyer with twenty years experience.

The selection of Associate Chief Justice Patrick LeSage to hear the high-profile case was also seen as judicial wisdom. LeSage, a former crown attorney, was known for his balance and calm during trials. It was said he ran his courtroom with an iron fist in a velvet glove.

Before the trial began, LeSage was juggling sensitive and opposing issues: the victims' families wanted the court cleared of media and public when the graphic videotapes were shown and details of their contents discussed; the media in turn wanted access to all the evidence and testimony. The French and Mahaffy families had filed a motion to close portions of the trial; the media opposed the motion. The CBC wanted to nationally televise the trial. LeSage quickly shot down the CBC request and, after the trial started, allowed only certain videos to be shown publicly. Only the jury and lawyers were permitted to see the French and Mahaffy assaults—the public gallery and the media would hear only the audio portions of the restricted videos.

THE VIDEOTAPES

The first weeks of the trial were the lead-up to the long-awaited appearance of Karla Homolka. Evidence of the sexual assaults on Tammy Homolka and a young woman identified only as "Jane Doe" were shown to the courtroom. The trails that led to the evidence surrounding the French and Mahaffy murders were laid out.

A horror show of videotape segments, which clearly tested their emotional barriers, were presented to the jury:

One videotape revealed the couple's assault on the unconscious Tammy Homolka. Bernardo and Karla and Tammy Homolka are seen drinking in the basement of the Homolka home. A towel soaked with halothane, an anesthetic, is held over the intoxicated and drugged teen's face; she is then raped by Bernardo. He next demands that Karla—who is upset because he isn't wearing a condom—perform sexual acts on Tammy. Karla protests, worrying that her parents, upstairs, might come down.

After resisting, she performs oral sex on her unconscious sister. On camera, Karla says that performing the act was "fucking disgusting."

Another scene, videotaped weeks after Tammy died, has the couple fantasizing about kidnapping and raping teenaged girls as they share confidences about the death of Tammy Homolka. One hour-long video features Homolka telling Bernardo to bring home girls, "virgins", as young as thirteen so that he can engage in sex with them.

"We can do it every weekend," says a naked Homolka, as they perform sex acts. "We can do it whenever we can," she says, because "I love you...because you're the king, because you deserve it."

Bernardo, also naked, asks if she will help him get virgins and Karla agrees: "Go in the car with you if you want. Or I'll stay here and I'll clean up afterwards, like I did on Sunday. I'll do everything I can 'cause I want to be happy, 'cause you're the king. I'm your keeper of virgins."

Bernardo then asks how Karla came up with the idea: "You told me something about it before. Is it because Tammy is gone?"

Karla: "It's the closest thing we can get to her...I would think that's part of the reason. But I also think we should make them ours." She later refers to Tammy as "our little virgin" and says: "I didn't give you my virginity so I gave you hers. I love you enough to do that....I loved it when you took her virginity."

In another portion of the tape recorded in Tammy's bedroom, Karla puts on her dead sister's clothing and, speaking in a schoolgirl's voice, pretends to be Tammy while she performs fellatio on Bernardo. Karla caresses his body with a long-stem rose and asks: "You know what we're going to do with this rose? We're going to give it to Tammy tomorrow. We'll go and put it on her grave." She refers to Bernardo's penis as "Snuffles" on several occasions.

Bernardo, lying on his back on Tammy's waterbed surrounded by Tammy's stuffed animals, with a pair of Tammy's underpants in his mouth, stares at a picture of the dead girl as Karla, her long blond hair covering her face, continues to fellate him. After a lengthy bout of oral sex, Bernardo climaxes, rolls over and says: "Oh Tam, we did it together." Karla, as Tammy, says: "I'm no longer a virgin." After Bernardo leaves the bed, Karla remains kneeling on the floor, grinning and waving at the videocamera.

Another videotape depicts the sexual assault of the drugged "Jane Doe," a young friend of the Bernardos'. Throughout the tape Bernardo is instructing Karla on controlling and monitoring the victim's movements.

Some of the most disturbing videotapes shown to the horrified jury were the ones depicting the sexual torture of 14-year-old Leslie Mahaffy. Her screams, on tape, echoed throughout the courtroom. In one videotape, Bernardo—sitting and sipping champagne—tells a bound, blindfolded and naked Leslie that the quality of her sexual performance could save her life: "The next two hours are going to determine what I do to you. I'm judging you right now, okay? Right now you're scoring perfect."

Leslie dissolves in terror and begs to be set free: "I want to see my brother and my friends," she cries, and then screams in pain. "Just let me go. I'll never tell ... I'll never double-cross you."

Both Bernardo and Karla sexually abuse the screaming teen.

"Who is your favorite guy right now? I think you know who I want you to say," he prompts Leslie.

"I want you," she answers.

Leslie is also videotaped urinating, getting undressed and washing herself. One twenty-five minute segment shows her kissing and performing oral sex on Karla Homolka. Watching, Bernardo moans in pleasure and tells Leslie: "You're in my good books." He then demands that Leslie perform analingus on him. "Make me feel good."

The final segment of the tape is taken in the master bedroom, with Leslie telling Bernardo, "I just want to do what you want."

"Good girl," Bernardo says and then anally rapes the kneeling teen who is bound hand and foot. Her screams are prolonged.

In the background of the video is a length of electrical cord; the device, Houlahan said, that was used minutes later to strangle her.

The savagery of the attack on 14-year-old Leslie Mahaffy was powerful enough that Justice LeSage, having said earlier each video would be shown three times, asked Houlahan not to replay it. LeSage apologized to the jury and sent them home: "It's not a pleasant way to end the week," he told them. "But that's the evidence."

After the weekend break, the jury was subjected to the videotaped agony and abuse suffered by Kristen French. In the videotapes, the spirited fifteen-year-old manages to hold on to her dignity as she's beaten, repeatedly raped, debased and used as a sex slave during the three days before her murder.

Following Bernardo's twisted script, Kristen carries out every sex act the couple demands of her. When she fails to bring Bernardo to orgasm, he pounds on her back and head: "You can't get me off...you're never going home if you don't," he tells her, adding that her performance would decide if she lived or died.

Kristen is told by both assailants to call Bernardo "the king" and "master." "You're the most powerful man in the whole world," she recites. "... I love you."

Karla praises the girl: "You're a good little sex slave, Kristen."

When Kristen loses her temper and calls him a "bastard," Bernardo takes her to an upstairs washroom, tries to defecate on her head, and then proceeds to urinate on her. Bernardo asks why she called him a bastard: "Who the fuck do you think you are?"

Ever polite, Kristen apologizes: "Pardon me?...I couldn't help myself...I'm sorry." Bernardo tells Karla to sexually assault her with a wine bottle. "It's okay if it hurts," he tells Karla.

One segment shows French performing a sex act on Bernardo: "Is it okay?"

Bernardo tells her, "Keep going, you're doing good."

Under his direction, the teen tells him she loves him twenty-six times. He directs both women to talk "some love stuff."

Karla: "I love you, Kristen."

Kristen responds with, "I love you, too."

An hour after that tape—in the words of Crown prosecutor Houlahan—Bernardo strangled Kristen.

Bernardo's defense team made few objections to the videotapes or to the accompanying testimony of Niagara Regional Police Sgt. Gary Beaulieu. Under cross-examination by Tony Bryant, Beaulieu disclosed that Homolka had been interviewed 58 days for a total of 200 hours. Bryant questioned the sergeant about the audio transcripts of the tapes, which took more than 900 man-hours to prepare. Beaulieu admitted there were some errors and unintelligible parts on the audio transcripts. Bryant then challenged the interpretations of these parts as well as the interpretations of what caused certain marks on the victims' bodies.

Expert Dr. Noel McAuliffe was called to testify about the forensics of the case. McAuliffe admitted that no cause of death could be found on Leslie Mahaffy's dismembered body; that Kristen French had been strangled; that Mahaffy had twin bruises on her back consistent with someone kneeling on her; that French had bruising on her wrists and ankles and about her head. On cross-examination, John Rosen suggested that Karla Homolka could easily have smothered Mahaffy with a pillow and that French could have accidentally choked herself while trying to free herself.

Referring to Homolka's videotaped comment, "Fucking disgusting," as she was told to perform oral sex on her sister, Rosen revealed the fact that Tammy was menstruating the night she died. He went on to suggest that, rather than the act itself, it was the taste of menstrual blood that Homolka found disgusting.

The rest of the week was taken up with testimony from an anesthetist (who said the alcohol, sleeping pills and halothane could have led to the death of Tammy Homolka) and details of the seventy-one-day police search of the Bayview Drive home. Two tapes of Bernardo—crying and screaming for Karla, who had recently left him—were also played.

The cross-examination chipped away at the evidence, splitting time-lines, and raising the possibility that Karla could have committed the murders.

But in spite of the aggressive nature of the cross-examination, Rosen was clearly saving his ammunition for what was called the "courtroom confrontation of the century": the examination of Karla Homolka.

KARLA'S TESTIMONY

On Monday, June 19, 1995, twenty-five-year-old Karla Homolka made her way to the witness box. Throughout her testimony, she kept her eyes focused on Houlahan, only occasionally glancing at her former husband sitting in the prisoner's dock. Looking demure, her long hair hanging straight and parted neatly on one side, Karla for the most part avoided Bernardo's small smiles and long probing stares.

Before she was examined, Judge LeSage told the jury that Karla Homolka's testimony was to be that of an accomplice and should be carefully assessed. "You should remember that she is involved. She participated in these crimes. She has been convicted of these crimes.…There is a natural inclination for one to lessen one's own involvement and point the finger at another," he said. "Particularly when one is involved in the crime. This is a matter of credibility for you to determine."

Karla's testimony led the jury through her early years. She told of their initial sexual encounter the day they met, and their closeness. "He treated me like a princess, like I was the only girl in the world...he was respectful of my parents. He brought me flowers."

She said their sex life was "basically normal vaginal intercourse," noting it was "good." Bernardo, she said, showered her with gifts and slowly became a powerful influence in her life. Because of him, she decided not to to go to university; instead she'd be a full-time mother to their children: "He just has this magnetism. It sounds stupid, but from that night I met him, I knew I would marry him. It's like, he has this power over women."

She said he wouldn't let her wear miniskirts to school, or go out with her friends to dances and social events. Bernardo, she testified, took over her life, making her submit to his whims. He became verbally abusive, repeatedly chastising her for her behavior.

The nature of their sex life changed within months. Karla began wearing dog-collars and handcuffs at his urging. While having sex, she was made to call herself a litany of demeaning names. Also at his urging, she began fellating him—although she found it unpleasant. His favorite sex act was anal intercourse: she didn't like that either but, again, she complied when he demanded. If she refused or failed to perform adequately, she said, he would fly into a rage and beat her.

He forced her to pose for obscene photographs, she said; photographs that were then introduced by Houlahan. In some, Karla is seen having sex with Bernardo while he holds a knife to her; a cord wrapped around her neck. In other photos, Karla is gagged and handcuffed.

Karla said Bernardo began suggesting bringing other women into their sex lives; he also wanted a sex slave. Shown photographs in which she is smiling, appearing to be having a good time, Karla said: "It wasn't all bad...Most of the time he treated me nicely." She said she didn't tell her parents of the problems she was having with Bernardo: "I was afraid of him, but part of me still loved him. He also told me not to air our dirty laundry. I didn't want my parents to know what he was doing to me—I still loved him..."

Houlahan brought forward a series of love notes and cards Karla had sent Bernardo, many offering unlimited sexual services. One card read: "Roses are red, violets are blue, there's nothing more fun, than a pervert like you." A note said: "Your little girl wants to be abused. She needs her big bad businessman to dominate her the best he can."

Of the drugging and raping of her sister, Karla said Bernardo often had her pretend to be Tammy during sex. "He would have me say, 'My name is Tammy, I'm fifteen-years-old, I'm your virgin. I love and I want to marry you'". She testified she went along with his plan to drug Tammy because "he told me it would only take five minutes…I finally agreed to it. Because I thought it would be a one-time thing and that nobody would get hurt."

On the day of the assault, two days before Christmas 1990, Bernardo said to Karla that Tammy would be "a great Christmas present for me." Later that night, Bernardo raped the teen vaginally and anally, refusing to wear a condom as he'd promised. Karla testified she was ordered to put her fingers in her unconscious sister's vagina and lick them. First she resisted, then gave in. Bernardo, videotaping the entire assault, hit her in the head for spoiling his tape after she said "fucking disgusting."

Soon after, Tammy Homolka began vomiting and stopped breathing. Karla cleaned up signs of the sex attack and called 911.

After Tammy's death, and needing time to grieve alone as a family, the Homolkas wanted Bernardo to leave their home. When Karla passed the news on to Bernardo, he flew into a rage, she said. "He felt rejected." And when the Homolkas, strapped for cash after burying Tammy, said they would have trouble financing Karla and Bernardo's wedding, he again became enraged, suggesting they should mortgage their home to pay for the wedding, Karla testified.

After the couple moved into the Bayview Drive home, Karla said, the violence escalated: "He said, 'Be ready for the nightly terrorist attacks.'" But this time, she said, she stayed with Bernardo because he had the incriminating tape of their assault on Tammy.

When Houlahan asked her who killed Leslie Mahaffy and Kristen French, Karla said, "Paul Bernardo…Paul strangled them with a black electrical cord." She said she was in the room, watching.

Karla testified that Bernardo brought Leslie home in the middle of the night in June 1991, after taking her from her backyard. The 14-year-old was raped and kept blindfolded. Bernardo interviewed her about her family, her hobbies and her school. Leslie was also raped vaginally and anally and forced to engage in sex acts with Homolka. Karla said Bernardo told her he'd have to kill Leslie. "And I asked him to reconsider," she told the court. But he said they'd go to jail for twenty-five years. Karla said she didn't want Leslie to feel pain, so she gave her drugs and a stuffed animal, a white teddy bear Bernardo had given her.

"Paul got an electrical cord from the basement and wrapped the ends around his hands," Karla told the jury. "He went over to her…and strangled her." The couple thought Leslie was dead, but a few minutes later she gasped for air. Bernardo, she said, strangled Leslie again, successfully. The body was stashed in the basement because the Homolkas were coming over to celebrate Father's Day.

Later, the body was cut into ten pieces, encased in cement and dumped into Lake Gibson. Karla said Bernardo, by himself, cut up the body with a saw in the basement. Afterwards, he said he "didn't want to eat meat for a long time," Karla told the court. "He said he couldn't believe how light the head was…he was laughing and joking about it."

In Hawaii, two weeks after the murder, Karla described their honeymoon as one "from hell" because of the beatings Bernardo inflicted on her.

Returning to Canada, the couple began stalking young women in the Niagara Region. "He had told me at some point that he used to do this without me," Karla told the court. "After we got married and he knew that he had me under his total control, he decided I should go with him." Bernardo talked of building a country home with a dungeon in the basement to keep young girls as sex slaves.

The physical and emotional abuse continued through the marriage, Karla claimed. She was assaulted with pieces of firewood, with shoes, a flashlight, car keys and the top of a lead-crystal wine decanter. "Anything that was within reach he would hit me with." When Bernardo whipped her as she knelt naked, she would say: "Please whip me, sir." Karla responded to her husband's assaults with love notes and vows of love and pleas for attention.

Of the day in April 1992 when they kidnapped Kristen French, Karla testified that although Bernardo was very excited, she was "just totally dead inside."

As Kristen had walked by the Grace Lutheran Church that day, Karla called her to their car and asked for directions. When Kristen came over, Karla pulled out a map, opened the car door and got out. Bernardo also exited the car, came around and flashed a knife at the teen: "You're coming with us." Karla jumped into the back of the car and Bernardo tried to force Kristen into the front passenger seat. The fifteen-year-old fought, calling him a bastard. Karla jumped into the backseat and when Kristen was finally forced into the vehicle, Karla grabbed her hair to keep her head down. The teen, wearing her Holy Cross school uniform, was taken to the Bayview Drive home where Karla unplugged all the phones and put a chain lock on the front door.

After being questioned about her family, her hobbies and her boyfriend, Kristen was forced to have sex with Karla and was anally raped by Bernardo. He promised her she could go home if she performed well. While performing fellatio on him, the teen was repeatedly pounded on the back by Bernardo. He demanded she denounce her boyfriend and call herself demeaning names. Bernardo directed a sex scene with Kristen wearing her school outfit and Karla wearing her dead sister's clothing. They were to pretend they were getting ready to go out on dates. Bernardo made a contest out of it: whoever wore the best perfume would not be anally assaulted. "Paul judged us," Karla testified. "He said Kristen was the winner because she had the nicest perfume, but he owed his wife preferential treatment." Kristen was anally raped.

During her first days in captivity, Kristen was polite and did everything she could to please Bernardo's fantasies. At one point she called him "the most powerful man in the whole world. All the girls at Holy Cross love you." Karla called her "a good little sex slave." But by the third day Kristen grew defiant: she refused to denounce her boyfriend and acted bored when Bernardo tried to show off his rap music skills. For this she was beaten.

When she called him a "bastard" she was put naked into an empty bathtub where Bernardo tried to defecate on her. He couldn't, but urinated on her instead. She was repeatedly ordered to tell him she loved him: she said "I love you" over and over.

On Easter Sunday, Karla testified, she knew Kristen would have to be killed: "Paul and I had to go to my parents' house for Easter dinner. He said he wanted to keep her longer so he could continue to use her as a sex slave. I told him we should go to my parents' home to establish an alibi."

Later in the day, Bernardo tried to get Kristen to perform fellatio but she wasn't cooperating. He beat her: "She acted like she didn't care," Karla told the court. Kristen told Bernardo, "Some things are worth dying for."

Bernardo showed the teen a video of Leslie Mahaffy. Kristen recognized the victim and, while she didn't appeared scared, began cooperating more with Bernardo's demands.

Later, Bernardo made her kneel in front of Karla's hope chest. He handed his wife a bottle and told her to put the bottle in the young girl's vagina. When Karla didn't do it as forcefully as he'd demanded, he took the bottle himself and continued the assault. Then he raped Kristen. Afterwards he again raped her, from behind, and with the electrical cord tied around Kristen's neck. He began talking to the teen about dying, then pulled the cord tight around her neck. "She started talking to him and was really calm," Karla said. "He cut her off in the middle of a word. He had it (the cord) wrapped around both hands and he pulled it tight in the middle of her talking."

Worried that she might lose consciousness, then revive as Mahaffy did, Bernardo kept the cord tight around French's throat and measured time off a digital clock: seven minutes.

After the murder, Bernardo went downstairs to shower; Karla went downstairs also, to blow-dry her hair. They then went to the

Homolkas' home for dinner, leaving Kristen's body on the bedroom floor. When they returned, they cut off Kristen's hair in case identifiable carpet fibres were caught in it, and washed the body in the Jacuzzi. Karla douched the body to clear out any semen left inside. The corpse had been left in a fetal position after the killing and rigor mortis had set in. Karla said her husband remarked it was a good thing Kristen had been lying fetal because it wouldn't fit into the hatchback of his car otherwise.

That night they dumped Kristen French's body in Burlington.

THE DEAL

On the final day of direct examination, Karla detailed the deal she'd made with the prosecutors in return for her twelve-year sentence in the Mahaffy-French killings. Among them: the deal would be terminated if it turned out she'd been culpable for any other deaths; she would give full statements in the death of Kristen French, Leslie Mahaffy and her sister, Tammy; she would help recover evidence of the crimes; she would testify against Bernardo; she wouldn't speak to the media or profit from the deaths of her sister, French or Mahaffy.

The Crown agreed not to interfere with any chance she had for early parole.

Throughout her testimony, Karla insisted she participated because she was afraid of Bernardo; that he would expose the tapes, particularly the one of her sister being raped, to her parents. She also said she feared becoming a victim of Bernardo's.

The main prongs of the Crown's case were the videotapes and Karla's testimony. The tapes showed all manner of sexual depravity but none showed murder. That Bernardo had killed the teens was all based on Karla's word.

THE CROSS-EXAMINATION OF KARLA

The showdown between John Rosen and Karla Homolka was expected to be high drama. And it didn't disappoint. The first day, after Homolka was seated in the witness box, Rosen was out of his chair and into her face with pictures of the three dead girls. He showed her Tammy Homolka's school picture, then flashed a photo of her in death: "That's your sister, Tammy, lying on a gurney," he said. "It's a picture you can't possibly forget."

Then he produced a school photo of Leslie Mahaffy; he followed it with a picture of her torso after it had been removed from the cement. Next was Kristen French, first in life, then a picture of her dead.

Karla appeared shaken by the frontal assault and Rosen's questions about her conscience, following each set of pictures. Rosen's attack was so energetic that Justice LeSage had to ask him several times to slow down so the court reporter could keep up with him.

In a more measured manner, Rosen took Karla through her first meeting with Bernardo, saying she'd had sex with him within an hour of meeting him. Karla protested, saying it was more like two hours.

He hammered at her: why didn't you leave Bernardo?; why didn't you tell someone what was going on?—the police, your parents? "Did you pick up the telephone and call the police and say, I want to speak to you about Kristen French, Leslie Mahaffy, and my sister, Tammy?" Rosen asked.

"No, I didn't."

"What you did was go out and have a heck of a time," Rosen said, quoting from an interview she gave police after she began cooperating: " 'I forgot about Tammy, I forgot about Leslie, and I forgot about Kristen. I forgot about everything. I made myself forget and I went out and had a great time.' "

Rosen pointed out several opportunities Karla had while the two victims were being held captive to flee the house and call police. He picked over the deal she later made with police and then detailed the love notes she'd written Bernardo; he also produced letters she'd written in which she disparaged her parents, calling them "assholes" because they couldn't afford the high cost of their daughter's planned wedding, especially after the expense of Tammy's funeral.

Rosen suggested Karla fed her sister sleeping pills in spaghetti sauce five months before the fatal Christmas assault so that Bernardo could rape her. Homolka fired back: "You're dead wrong."

He said Karla picked Kristen French as a victim—"...she was the kind of tall, slim, dark-haired girl that you like"—because she wanted a "play-toy" for the weekend. He said she smothered Leslie Mahaffy with a pillow and that she was present in the basement when Bernardo dismembered her corpse. He said she killed French with a mallet when the victim tried to escape from the Bayview Drive home while Bernardo was out getting food: "She tried to go to the bathroom and she came after you with a shove and you went after her with the mallet, didn't you?" Rosen charged. Karla denied all the charges and said: "That's a total lie. I never hit her with the mallet."

Karla constantly responded to Rosen's questions by saying she did everything at Bernardo's direction, or by flatly denying the defence allegations.

Finally, after seventeen days of examination and cross-examination, it was over. Karla left the courtroom, had a brief visit with her parents, and was whisked to downtown 51 Division where she was transferred to an air-conditioned van with tinted windows for her trip back to prison. Whether she'd managed to successfully fend off Rosen's aggressive attack, whether the jury believed Rosen's alternate theory, was the matter of some debate.

And then there were the intriguing hints that came up during Rosen's cross-examination: two broad hints that his client would taken the stand.

BERNARDO IN THE BOX

On August 15, John Rosen rose and spoke eleven words that answered the weeks of heightening speculation: "Members of the jury, I call to the stand Paul Bernardo."

Rosen went right to the heart of his defence, that Bernardo and Karla lived in a two-story house: her story and his story.

At times testifying with the demeanor of a professional

witness, angling his body towards the jury and directing many of his answers to them, Bernardo quickly admitted to being a kidnapper and a sadistic rapist. But he denied being a murderer. Both Mahaffy and French had died when they were alone with Karla, he told the court.

Conservatively dressed in a blue suit, white shirt and tie, he told the jury, "People, I know I've done some really terrible things...I'm really sorry for that and I know I deserve to be punished...but I didn't kill these girls."

During direct examination by Rosen, Bernardo said Karla was not his victim but, rather, an equal partner in kinky sex from the beginning of their relationship: "All we'd do when I went down there [to St. Catharines, to visit Karla] is we'd drink and we'd have sex. It was worth the drive down." He said he liked her to wear a metal-studded dog collar and spout comments like "I'm just a fucking dog" when they were having sex.

Of Tammy Homolka, he said that once, while at a bar, he and the teenager got drunk and ended up necking and fondling each other. When they returned home, Karla was jealous. Later, in July, he said, Karla spiked spaghetti sauce and fed it to Tammy: "I pulled Tammy's pants down and entered her, and I was in for about a minute. Karla was there watching and as soon as I finished, Tammy started to wake up so we both went out of the room." The couple made other attempts to drug and rape Tammy.

Bernardo admitted to a previously unknown abduction and rape in January 1991 of a teenaged hitchhiker. He testified that he'd brought the girl to the Homolkas' home, blindfolded, for three-way sex but that Karla was afraid to join in because the victim was combative. The hitchhiker was later released on a side street in St. Catharines.

He denied strangling Leslie Mahaffy and Kristen French with a black electrical cord, as Karla had testified. He said he'd planned to turn the fourteen-year-old loose at a plaza near her home, but that Karla had some concerns about whether or not the girl had seen him. He said he went out to prepare his car to drop off Mahaffy, leaving her alone with Karla. When he went back inside, Mahaffy was lying face down on a pillow, not breathing. He also said that, contrary to her testimony, Karla had been present as he dismembered the body. According to Bernardo, Karla covered the basement windows with towels and washed Leslie Mahaffy's body parts after the dismemberment. Both of them wore old clothes; he also donned a hat and goggles for the grisly deed.

Bernardo testified that it was Karla who spotted Kristen French in April 1992 as there were out shopping and said: "How about grabbing one for the night?" Again Bernardo gave Karla a more prominent role in the kidnapping and rapes, but acknowledged, in a calm voice, his abuse of the victim: he did anally rape her as punishment. But he denied strangling French. He went out for food, he said, leaving the victim with Karla. When he returned, he found his wife crying. She said: "Kristen tried to escape."

"I ran upstairs and saw her and she was dead," he testified, adding French was lying face down with her hands cuffed and a cord around her neck. "I said, 'My God, what happened?' Karla said she'd 'wanted to escape…I didn't mean to do it.' I said, 'I know.' "

He chose not to dismember the body, as he had with Mahaffy's: "That was one of the most disgusting things I'd ever done."

Winding down his examination, Rosen asked his client if he'd changed since he was arrested. Bernardo responded: "When I look back at how our sex fantasies hurt so many people, I can't believe I was the same person."

Prosecutor Ray Houlahan was quick at Bernardo, running a portion of video in which Kristen French is being raped. Dramatically, he ordered a frame frozen: it showed Bernardo's face twisted with rage. "That's the face of a killer, isn't it?" he asked.

Houlahan picked through the videotapes, at one point eliciting Bernardo's reason for keeping the tapes. "It was the last memory of these girls' lives...they were a significant part of events in our life. We would watch them to remember," he said.

When queried, Bernardo admitted he enjoyed raping Leslie Mahaffy as she screamed. He also admitted to threatening to kill the teen if she didn't defecate for him and agreed it was his decision whether or not Kristen French left the Bayview Drive home alive.

But he stuck to his assertion that Karla wasn't some kind of a programmed zombie; that she was a "secondary boss" and that she killed Mahaffy and French.

At one point, a bitter wave of laughter went through the courtroom when Bernardo admitted he had a problem with his sexuality: "Down the road, I'm going to have to seek professional help for it."

In their closing arguments, both John Rosen and Ray Houlahan staked out their positions. Rosen's was simple: While his client was everything from a depraved rapist to a deranged kidnapper, he was no murderer. The deaths of Leslie Mahaffy and Kristen French were, he argued, something less than first-degree murder—manslaughter, maybe. Houlahan rejected any notion that Bernardo was anything but a cold-blooded killer entirely guilty of two counts of first degree murder.

It took the jury just six hours to bring Bernardo in guilty on all nine counts. Bernardo was automatically sentenced to life in prison with no eligibility for parole for 25 years. Judge LeSage ordered him back to court September 15 for sentencing on the remaining charges.

And with the end of the murder trial, Bernardo was still before the courts on several charges related to the brutal serial rapist attacks that terrorized east Metro in the late 1980s.

BIKERS COAST TO COAST

MONTREAL WAS ROCKED by bombs and bullets as biker gang violence claimed several lives and left dozens wounded—including a freelance journalist—during a turf war for control of the city's illicit drug trade.

The Rock Machine and their rivals, the Rockers, began the serious phase of the struggle in October 1994. Six people died as the groups opened fire on one another and set off powerful bombs.

On December 5, 1994, a Rock Machine member was blown up when the bomb he was carrying in a stolen car went off by accident in Longueuil. On January 15, 1995, another Rock Machine member was tinkering with a bomb in a stolen van in the city's east end when it, too, went off accidentally. The Rock Machiner was wearing a flak jacket but might as well have been wearing a bathing suit: detectives didn't even recover a finger to print after the blast.

A short time later police in Longueuil seized a van containing more than ten kilos of dynamite and thousands of nails to be used as shrapnel.

A biker, a member of a gang associated with the Hell's Angels, lost both legs when a car bomb was set off near his home.

Police set up a task force and arrested eighty gang members on more than two hundred charges.

The Rockers operated from a fortified house, complete with cinder block walls and surveillance cameras. Their security wasn't quite a hundred percent: in early March the gang found a bomb in front of their house. They called the police bomb squad to remove it. On March 17 an explosive was tossed onto the doorstep from a passing van, blowing out the clubhouse's bulletproof windows and shattering glass in several nearby houses.

There was outrage over that bombing and over reports that the house had been paid for through a $105,000 mortgage from the Federal Business Development Bank.

And the battle wasn't confined to the streets. Several Rockers and Rock Machine members intentionally got themselves arrested so they could get sent to the Bordeaux jail in Montreal's north end to help imprisoned members fight for control of the jail's lucrative drug business.

Free-lance journalist Robert Monastesse opened the door of his suburban home in mid-February and was shot through both legs by an unknown gunman. Monastesse, who has written extensively about the biker wars, was placed under police protection.

Police said several bike gangs are involved in the ongoing struggle. They note that it isn't just the drug trade at stake. Gun smuggling, prostitution, money laundering and cross-border criminal operations are all up for grabs.

As well, intelligence detectives allege the Angels are vying for a piece of the Ontario drug trade, as senior members of the Angels have been surveilled as they visited underworld haunts in Metro Toronto.

Quebec police said in early April they'd forced a truce in the biker gang war with the arrests of thirteen Hell's Angels and associates for more than a dozen murders. Suspects were picked up in a series of raids in Quebec City and Trois-Rivières. Fifteen guns were seized, including a submachine gun and rifles equipped with telescopic sights. Cocaine and cash were also seized. Police said more arrests, as many as ten, were expected.

An international money-laundering probe also netted some members of the Hell's Angels gang. The multimillion-dollar scheme involved the bikers and several Montreal people tied to the Italian underworld. Angels from Quebec and London, England, were picked up in what was called the largest money-laundering probe in Canadian history. Police said 558 kilograms of cocaine sold by the Colombians to Hell's Angels in England were seized.

Hell's Angels in British Columbia are a gold-plated concern that deserves a spot at the top of any Fortune 500 list.

The September 1994 *RCMP Gazette* decreed: "The Canadian Hell's Angels in B.C. are reputed to be the wealthiest chapters in the world."

So wealthy are the British Columbia Angels, says the *Gazette*, that other chapters were asked not to continuously ask for money from the western Canadians.

Real estate, stocks and a wide range of other legitimate business are part of the Angels' portfolio, RCMP reported.

The *Vancouver Sun* listed several businesses the Angels operate. These include a major grocery store, a travel agency, a cedar shakes and logging company, apartment buildings and motorcycle shops. Also listed were an Italian restaurant, a trucking company, a limousine service and a waste removal firm.

In a March 1995 interview with the *Vancouver Sun*, four members of the British Columbia Hell's Angels denied any ties to organized crime, and they accused the police of harassing them. "They also charged the media with aiding the RCMP in a smear campaign that is hurting bikers who are respectable business and family men," the *Sun* reported.

BIG CIRCLE BOYS KEEP GETTING BIGGER

Cross Canada—1994

Canada continues to be a primary target of the Big Circle Boys, a loosely knit organization of criminals from mainland China.

The BCBs, so named because their criminal network is made up of former political prisoners from a circle of detention centers around Guangzhou, operate sophisticated heroin, counterfeiting and credit-card-fraud rings.

Several Circle members were nabbed by Asian-crime detectives across Canada and most were found to be refugees or refugee claimants, intelligence files show.

Among the cases probed:

- In December 1994 a gang was found operating in Metropolitan Toronto, where they ran a fraud scheme by placing ads in Chinese newspapers seeking office help. During interviews, the victims filled out applications giving personal information. The information was then used by the gangsters to obtain credit cards, bank loans and false documents.

- In November 1994 Toronto police found one of the highest-ranking BCB bosses among five people arrested in the extortion of a wealthy Chinatown businessman. The boss, a federal government employee, demanded cash from the businessman. When the businessman refused, he was beaten. Asian investigators were called in, and the extortionists were arrested as they tried to collect the payoff. Detectives also discovered that gang members were making loans; interest was one hundred percent a week.
- A joint Canada–Republic of China investigation led to the arrests in July of four men for peddling phony credit cards and Ontario drivers' licenses. The arrests were part of a worldwide fight against the gang's multimillion-dollar credit-card network. Police seized a laminating machine, stencils, blank licenses and credit cards and several thousand dollars in Canadian and U.S. currency. Canada Customs officers in Vancouver seized two packages from China in early June; they also seized bundles of false credit cards.
- In June 1994 the BCBs were nabbed just west of Metro Toronto where they were operating a credit-card scam. Police seized an Uzi submachine gun and thousands of dollars in high-quality bogus twenty-dollar bills. Police estimated half the counterfeit twenties in circulation were from the BCB ring.
- Two BCB gangs were rounded up in April 1994 as a result of another international probe, ranging from Asia to North and South America. Again police seized credit cards and paraphernalia linked to wide-scale fraud. Seventeen gangsters were picked up.
- The Canadian Bankers Association estimated credit-card losses worldwide are a billion-dollar headache. Several other members of the gang have been arrested for credit-card fraud in major centers across Canada.
- RCMP experts believe the gang is prominent in the worldwide heroin trade; they cite several arrests and seizures in Vancouver and Toronto.

THE TRAGEDY OF LOLITA SANTAMARIA

Toronto—February 1994

A Toronto area woman who slashed her children's wrists before trying to kill herself in the same fashion was acquitted of attempted murder. Lolita Santamaria, forty-one, pleaded guilty to assault and was sentenced to one day in jail plus time served.

Court was told Santamaria attacked her children on February 10, 1994, slashing at their wrists and slicing her own wrist after learning her husband, Reynaldo, was having an affair with her niece.

Santamaria was charged and spent fifteen months awaiting trial. While she was in jail, she learned that Reynaldo had moved in with the niece. She began seeking custody, child support and alimony.

During her trial, Santamaria was described as a "model mother" by her lawyer, David Maubach: "Her parenting abilities are beyond question. She never led a criminal life. Remember, what she did to her children, she also did to herself."

Santamaria said she'll fight for custody or access to the children.

HANGING JUSTICE

Kingston—March 1994

Triple killer Terrence Fitzsimmons was found dead in his Kingston Penitentiary cell on March 29, 1994.

Fitzsimmons, thirty, had hung himself from his cell bars.

The London, Ontario, man was serving a twenty-five-year sentence after pleading guilty to the murders of Toronto dentist Norman Rasky, Montreal cabbie Fernand Talbot and Fitzsimmons's partner-in-crime Don Hebert.

Fitzsimmons and Hebert, later described in court as "the brotherhood of doom," were drug users who committed robberies to pay for their habits. They went on a murder spree in 1993, beginning in Toronto with the beating death of Rasky, a member of the city's gay community. After the Rasky slaying, the killers fled to Montreal where they murdered Talbot. In a suicide pact, with police closing in, Fitzsimmons fatally stabbed his partner behind an abandoned Ottawa restaurant. He later turned himself in to police.

While in jail Fitzsimmons made a videotaped statement through his lawyer, saying he'd injected himself with HIV-tainted blood to punish himself. "I knew society wouldn't be satisfied with this sentence, so I thought I'd give them the capital punishment they always wanted."

JOE MACDONALD

Sudbury—March 1994

Two cop killers got life in prison for murdering Sudbury policeman Joe MacDonald. But the end of the trial on March 4, 1994, was the start of a storm of controversy aimed at the parole system.

Clinton Cuzack and Peter Pennett, both thirty, were found guilty of first-degree murder and were sentenced to life in prison.

Court was told MacDonald, twenty-nine, made a routine traffic stop during the early morning hours on October 7, 1993. He was attacked by Cuzack and Pennett, pistol-whipped and shot five times. Three bullets were fired into his brain. MacDonald managed to wound Cuzack three times. During the shooting spree, Cuzack hit his accomplice in the wrist.

After a fifty-two-day trial in which each of the two accused tried to hang the shooting on the other, both were convicted of first-degree murder. Spectators in the courtroom burst into cheers.

The cheers quickly turned to anger when police officers and MacDonald's widow and mother of his two infant children demanded to know why the Ontario Parole Board freed Cuzack from Millbrook Prison a few months before the murder. The violent drug dealer had thirty convictions on his record and had been refused parole amid warnings from police and parole officials in May 1993. But three months later he was freed by the board. He went to a halfway house on August 26 but walked away two weeks later.

The case sparked outrage against Ontario's NDP-dominated parole board, and Opposition members called for the firing of chairman Don Wadel.

In the midst of the controversy a similar case erupted in Longlac, when OPP officer Dan Kotanko suffered through a shootout and hostage-taking involving another parolee. James Christopher Debruin—whose status in prison had increased from medium to high-risk—had been freed from Millbrook maximum security prison on January 26 after serving five months of a fifteen-month sentence for dangerous driving and car theft. Released to a halfway house, Debruin fled. Twelve days later, Kotanko and his partner, Constable Byron Horneck, got into a struggle with car thieves. Kotanko was shot and wounded. The thieves got away and took two truck drivers hostage. Debruin was nabbed at a police roadblock.

The heat from the high-profile cases took its toll: Wadel was sacked by Ontario Solicitor General David Christopherson. The firing came the same day as a coalition of police associations was to make a formal demand for Wadel's ouster.

NO ESCAPE IN DEATH

Toronto—May 1994

The family of murder victim Elsie Sinclair was outraged to find the killer of the Metro Toronto woman would be buried just fifteen meters from her grave.

Sinclair, twenty-nine, was shot dead February 10 by Tyrone Benjamin, who then took his own life. The victim and her killer had dated for several weeks leading up to the slaying. Benjamin, twenty-eight, of Montreal, pawned the woman's gold jewelry and gambled the money away. On February 10, police found them both dead, she of gunshots to the chest and he of a self-inflicted wound to the head.

Two days after Elsie Sinclair was buried, members of her family returned to the cemetery. They learned he would be buried at Beechwood Cemetery, as well, just fifteen meters away. They complained to the manager of the cemetery, who asked

Benjamin's family if they would let him dig another grave, promising not to hold up their ceremony.

They refused, saying they were in the middle of a funeral procession. The killer and his victim lay in the same row of unmarked graves until May 12 when, as a result of a court order, Benjamin's body was exhumed and moved to another cemetery.

"The grieving process will now be able to begin properly," said Michelle Lingi, lawyer for Sinclair's seventy-year-old father, Hugh.

ELLIOT LAKE MURDER–SUICIDE

Elliot Lake—May 1994

A deteriorating marriage turned into suicide and a desperate hunt for a little girl in the northern Ontario town of Elliot Lake in May 1994.

Katie Lynn Brosseau

After eight years of marriage Richard and Lynn Brosseau were in the midst of breaking up. The couple's daughter, two-and-a-half-year-old Katie Lynn, was caught in the middle.

On the Victoria Day long weekend, Richard, an avid hunter and outdoorsman, took his daughter on a camping trip. At the end of the weekend, Richard Brosseau's pickup truck was found in a wooded area on the outskirts of town. Inside was his body and his recently fired hunting gun. There was no sign of Katie Lynn.

Brosseau's suicide was shocking, but hardly surprising. His father and two uncles had killed themselves. Brosseau had become despondent when he lost his job at a local mine that was shut down and his marriage began coming apart the previous winter. Recognizing that he was deteriorating, his mother had persuaded him to get psychological counseling and to resume attending mass.

But he seemed to go from bad to worse. The Sunday before the ill-fated Victoria Day weekend, Richard had threatened to do what he apparently wound up doing: to kill himself and the child so he could take her to heaven to meet her grandfather.

A note written by Richard was found: "If I can't have her, she [Lynn] can't have her." And he vowed to "take her to a better place" and take care of her. He'd hide the body, he said, so it wouldn't be found and Lynn would suffer eternally.

After Richard's body was discovered, a massive search of the rugged countryside was kicked off, the largest in Elliot Lake's history. The downtown area was covered with purple ribbons as residents held out a ray of hope the child would be found alive.

The case came to a close near the end of the month when fishermen Dan Potvin and Steven Amyotte, investigating a broken-down dock, saw what they thought was a doll floating in Vermilion Lake near Sudbury, two hours away from where Brosseau had committed suicide.

It was Katie Lynn Brosseau's body, fully dressed. Police said there was no sign of violence to the little girl; she had been drowned.

Lynn Brosseau buried her daughter: "She was my daughter but it seems now that she's everyone's daughter....She will never be forgotten in this town."

Constable Todd Baylis

Clinton Junior Gayle

THE MURDER OF TODD BAYLIS

POLICEMAN'S SON MET policeman's son at 10:00 p.m., June 15, 1994, a hot Thursday, at an apartment building in the north end of Toronto. Seconds later one was dying of gunshot wounds and the other, hit by police gunfire, was on his way to a hospital and a first-degree murder charge.

Constable Todd Baylis died in surgery at 4:07 a.m., the result of a point-blank gunshot wound to the head. Clinton Junior Gayle recovered from his wounds and was later transferred to the Don Jail, where he's awaiting trial.

In the simplest equation, a crime had been committed and a suspect was before the courts. It could have ended there, indeed it might have, except for the scorching body temperature of the city.

The death of a policeman in the line of duty makes the thin blue line a little thinner. Every Canadian community that experiences the trauma of a cop killing goes through a convulsion: at root, people feel, "We lost one of the good guys." Police officers are on edge; the public is a little less lippy when they're stopped for speeding or have contact with an officer. Huge crowds of police officers and citizens attend formal, solemn funerals. In time, the public forgets. The cops don't. But for a while there's a cohesiveness between police and the public: the public realizes what police officers—who they usually only meet over a disputed traffic ticket—risk; the police realize that the public—not shy about parceling out a piece of their mind over the same ticket—cares. It's an awful way for two groups to understand each other, but what's already a tragedy would become unbearable if something positive didn't come out of it.

But it isn't always so.

Todd Baylis was twenty-five years old when he died. Three and a half years on the job, Baylis worked in uniform out of 12 Division, not one of the "hot" areas, but not Sleepy Hollow, either. A lot of the business for 12 Division officers was drug-related, and the trade was centered around a few specific apartment buildings in the area.

On June 16 Baylis was on his first shift, three in the afternoon to eleven, after returning from vacation. He and Mike Leone left their cruiser and were doing a routine walk-through of an apartment complex on Trethewey Drive, in an area where drug trafficking was a problem.

The officers opened a stairwell door and confronted a man they'd noticed in the area earlier.

"What's up?" Baylis asked the man.

Instead of answering, the man knocked Baylis down, sparking a foot pursuit. The suspect ran into the basement, then ended up at a locked door. He turned on Baylis and Leone. Leone told the man to stop and to lie on the ground. When he didn't, Leone pulled his pepper spray and fired into the man's face. Instead of subduing him, the spray seemed to make him angrier. With both officers following, the man climbed a flight of stairs and got outside the building. He pulled a 9mm Walther semiautomatic handgun, and as Baylis ran through the door, he fired a single shot into the officer's head. The bullet entered Baylis's head at the base of his right sideburn. Leone was fired on twice; one bullet hit his bulletproof vest, the other entered his back. Leone unleashed a volley of gunfire at the shooter, hitting him in the leg, arm and upper chest. The gunman continued to fire, but his gun jammed.

Both officers lay collapsed on the ground; the gunman lay near them. As police cruisers and ambulances screamed to the scene, area residents began gathering around. Some began shouting "racism" and "let the cop die" as police and paramedics attended the gravely wounded Baylis.

"The tension was unbelievable," *Toronto Star* reporter Peter Edwards said. Edwards, who'd sped to the scene from downtown after hearing the calls for "assist PC" and "officer down" on his police scanner, remembers a young Jamaican man telling him: "It's going to be harder to be black in this town.... Everybody'll look at me like I pulled the trigger."

Baylis, showing no vital signs, was rushed to hospital. He was revived and put on life support systems at Sunnybrook Medical Centre. He died about five hours later.

Leone was taken by police car to Humber Memorial Hospital, treated and released.

Accused shooter Clinton Junior Gayle, twenty-five, was taken to St. Michael's Hospital where he was kept under heavy police guard. He was charged with first-degree murder, attempted murder and possession of narcotics.

At 12 Division the grief was palpable. Metro Police Chief Bill McCormack, having stopped at Sunnybrook, gathered the officers together at 12 Division and spoke quietly to them. An officer who was present said McCormack, who ranks as one of the most popular police chiefs the force has ever had, was "quiet, low-keyed, very calming" during the meeting. "He was the sympathetic father, the understanding boss, the perfect policeman," the officer said.

Ted Baylis, the slain officer's father and a detective at 31 Division, was notified while on holiday in Florida. He jumped into his car and sped nonstop back to Toronto. He told the *Toronto Sun*, "Todd was more than just a son. He was my buddy. He was one of the nicest kids you'll ever meet. If he walked up here right now, you'd just love him."

Metro Toronto Police and some segments of the black community exist in a constant state of bitterness and hatred. Several police shootings of blacks have led to a widening chasm between the two groups. More extreme members of the organized black community have accused Metro officers of racism; some have called the entire force racist. The police services board, influenced by a left-wing provincial government, at times appeared to officers to be diametrically opposed to their interest, and safety. Some board members believe the police force is a paramilitary organization that must be dragged into the twentieth century. Chief McCormack had spent all of 1994 and part of 1995 locked in a constant struggle with board chair Susan Eng before retiring.

So the anger felt by most officers toward the cries of racism by a few of the bystanders at the Baylis murder site was part of a larger, more pervasive atmosphere of antagonism that never quite went away. But it was quickly put into perspective by a young black police officer, a friend of Baylis's, who told the *Toronto Sun*'s Christie Blatchford: "It's so ludicrous. Those people are obvious assholes. But because they're black, because the suspect is black, that's not a reflection of the real black community.…They don't represent me, they don't represent my parents."

The public, too, had their say. Flowers and cards poured in to 12 Division in the days after the shootings. Patrolling officers were stopped by residents of the Trethewey housing project and given expressions of sympathy.

A full-dress police funeral was attended by thousands of officers from across North America, and a memorial was placed at 12 Division in honor of Baylis.

By then the twin wild cards of race and immigration were dealt into an already tragic situation. When Clinton Gayle's background emerged, there was fury.

Gayle, the son of a Jamaican police superintendent, came to Canada with his mother and brother when he was nine years old.

By the time Clinton Gayle was charged in Baylis's slaying, he had more than a dozen criminal convictions, many for drug and weapons offenses.

The Metro Police Black Organized Crime Squad noted that he was a member of a powerful Jamaican posse; in his file he was called dangerous. His file also said he was often armed and involved in drug trafficking.

Gayle was first ordered deported in 1991 after being convicted of drug possession and trafficking, but he slipped through the immigration system. He continued to collect criminal convictions.

When Gayle's past came to light it sparked widespread anger among police officers. The Metro Police Association collected thousands of pledges from the public and launched a class-action suit against the Immigration Department, charging that they did not carry out their "statutory obligations" when they failed to deport Gayle.

Both the lawsuit and Gayle's criminal trial are pending.

Immigration Minister Sergio Marchi set up a twenty-member task force to track down wanted deportees. Marchi was responding to Gayle's background, and also to news that a suspect in the April 1994 shooting death of Georgina "ViVi" Leimonis was on a five-year deportation stay.

In March 1995, as Gayle waited to go to trial, a scandal rocked 12 Division and the entire police force. Four officers, some of them involved in the Baylis–Gayle case, were charged with planting drugs on suspects.

Crown officers and senior police fear the 12 Division scandal will affect the prosecution of Clinton Gayle.

HERO NABS ROLEX THIEF

Ottawa—June 1994

As a civil servant, Rene Garneau makes one hell of a wrestler.

The employee of the Solicitor General's Office was walking on the Sparks St. Mall in Ottawa in June 1994 when he heard a commotion behind him. He turned and heard someone yelling, "Thief! Stop him! Thief!"

Garneau spotted a heavyset youth running toward him and gave him a shoulder block, taking him to the ground. Garneau latched a headlock onto the youth and, with other passersby pinning the suspect's arms and legs, held him for police.

It turned out the seventeen-year-old had gone into Howard Manufacturing Jewellers and ripped off a six-thousand-dollar Rolex.

When the shop's owner, Howard Appotive, expressed his thanks to Garneau with an offer of a deal on jewelry, Garneau refused, saying he wanted a new pair of pants to replace the ones that got ripped during the citizen's arrest.

BIKER GANG TURF WARS

Ottawa—July 1994

A turf war between biker gangs over control of the Ontario drug trade spilled into the Ottawa area when a member of the Outlaws motorcycle gang found a bomb in the backyard of the clubhouse in July 1994.

On July 14, at 1:55 a.m., Ottawa police received an emergency call from a gang member reporting that a bomb had gone off. Officers went to the heavily fortified clubhouse on Ladouceur Street and found a partially exploded device. The incident was the second in the city in 1994: on April 12 the clubhouse was the target of a car bomb. No one was injured in either incident.

Police believe a power struggle is under way as some members of Ontario gangs fight to keep control of criminal activities in the face of a powerful move by Hell's Angels in Quebec.

The feud between the Outlaws and the Angels dates back to the mid-1970s, when two Angels were executed by an Outlaw in Florida. Since then, bombings and shootings have claimed several members on both sides. The body of one victim, an Ottawa Outlaws associate, was found welded into an oil drum in Kingston, Ontario.

JEAN BRUSH: A TALE OF MERCY

Hamilton—August 1994

A woman who killed her Alzheimer-stricken husband to end his life of "nightmarish hell" received a suspended sentence in a Hamilton, Ontario, court.

Jean Brush, eighty, pleaded guilty to manslaughter in the stabbing death of her blind husband of fifty-eight years, Cecil. Cecil, a retired steelworker, had asked his wife to kill him, the court was told.

"He said, 'Jean please, please do something, do something!'" she said. "I said, 'if I am going to do something, I am going to do it to myself as well. I want you and me to be together.'"

Cecil tried to stab himself, and she helped him before turning the weapon on herself.

Cecil Brush, eighty-one, was found dead in August 1994 of a knife wound to the chest. Jean Brush was found suffering from five self-inflicted wounds. She underwent surgery and survived.

She left a suicide note that read: "We lived our lifetime and it must end before we both become vegetables."

Brush's lawyer, Frank Genesee, said she was "a pioneer in the difficult area of euthanasia." He described her action as "an act of love" and asked for a suspended sentence. Crown Attorney David Carr agreed.

Judge Bernd Zabel told a somber courtroom Mrs. Brush's incarceration was pointless: "She has already suffered a harsher sentence—losing her husband," he said. "Her cries of help went unanswered.…It was a desperate attempt…so he could die with dignity."

He put Brush on probation for eighteen months and ordered her to seek the medical treatment advised by her doctor.

After the hearing, Brush told reporters her husband "was beyond hope."

"I tried to get him into a nursing home but I realized it wouldn't do him any good. I just hope there will be more help available for others."

UNDERWORLD STINGS

NEW-WAVE POLICING led to several successful sting operations against the underworld as Canadian investigators used innovative techniques to penetrate criminal organizations.

In September 1994, RCMP officers shut down a four-year probe dubbed Operation CCC that targeted the Italian Mafia, motorcycle gangs and white-collar criminals.

Operation CCC has become a legendary bit of street theater. Rather than running around trying to catch up with criminals and their cash, the Mounties opened a posh exchange house on Peel Street, in the center of Montreal's money-changing district. Equipped with hidden cameras and microphones, the Centre International Monétaire de Montréal (CIMM) became a magnet for bandits.

Putting the word out through informants and underworld sources, the Mounties let it be known the CIMM was operating a full business service for the mob, from money laundering to money exchanging.

The friendly, helpful staff at CIMM cheerfully accepted $65 million in criminal profits, mostly from the drug trade. "They'd bring money in boxes and suitcases," RCMP Staff-Sergeant Yvon Gagnon said. It was converted into U.S. funds, which police traced through two hundred bank accounts in Canada, the United States, South America and overseas.

When Operation CCC was brought to a halt, dozens of people were arrested, including Mafia members, Hell's Angels, lawyers and businessmen. Records were seized from more than thirty companies. Investigators seized accounts where they suspected criminal profits were being held and went after assets bought with the money.

So successful was the CIMM front that the undercover officers were asked to help smuggle a huge load of cocaine from Colombia to Canada. The officers obliged. They chartered a freighter, sailed to Colombia and picked up 558 kilos of drugs, which they brought to Montreal.

And the CIMM itself? It operated so well it could have made a profit, even during the current recession.

In June 1994 a cross-Canada sting by the RCMP's proceeds-of-crime teams cracked the glass ceiling between the underworld and the legitimate overworld that moves their profits.

In the drug underworld, American money talks, everything else walks. A key step in the movement of dirty money is to get profits into U.S. currency. Enter currency exchanges, which are required by law to record any transaction of more than a thousand dollars; as well, the customer has to prove his or her identity.

Posing as drug traffickers, RCMP proceeds-of-crime agents hit currency exchanges across Canada, exchanging Canadian money for U.S. bills. Seven cities were targeted: Victoria, Vancouver, Calgary, Edmonton, Toronto, Montreal and Quebec City.

The undercover operators, often posing as drug traffickers, visited several exchanges and successfully changed more than $3 million into U.S. funds without being asked to complete the required documentation. Almost two hundred charges were laid, involving thirty-six corporations and sixty-five individuals.

"Shady currency exchanges are an important link in the flow of illegal profits out of the country," said RCMP Superintendent Wayne Blackburn, who heads the Toronto proceeds-of-crime unit.

The company was called Grayson Transport Ltd., a Division of MIS. The company's logo was a chess piece, the knight's head.

If any of the bandits targeted by Project Atom had asked, they might have been told that MIS stood for Metro Intelligence Service, and that the knight's head was a police logo.

But nobody asked.

Project Atom ran for six years, one of the longest and most successful undercover projects ever. Four investigators penetrated the underworld and got next to the city's criminal elite.

The four undercover officers, three men and a woman, posed as small-time crooks who worked as truckers. They practised driving eighteen-wheel transport trucks at night at a Metro-area landfill site.

"From our standpoint in Canada, it's as deep as we've ever gone," said Staff-Inspector Ron Sandelli, who headed the intelligence squad.

On at least two occasions, according to Detective Gary Carter, who ran the operation, the undercover agents were confronted by the suspects who accused them of being police. But the officers kept their cool and shrugged, "If you don't like us, just walk away."

He said investigators got their biggest laughs as the mobsters discussed the police. "Their biggest joke was what they thought was the ineptness of the police," Carter told the *Toronto Star*. "They'd say the police have been trying to get us for years. They were thumbing their noses at the police all of the time, and we were right under their noses."

So close did the agents get that they were asked to sponsor a soccer team run by a major mobster. For two seasons the mobster proudly wore a knight's head on his soccer jersey, not knowing it was the Intelligence Squad logo.

During the six-year run of the undercover operation, police laid charges relating to murder conspiracy, weapons, fraud against governments, counterfeiting, theft, drugs, gaming and money laundering.

THE GIRL IN THE SUITCASE

Toronto—September 1994

A lengthy homicide probe by York Regional Police has left them with more questions than answers.

Detectives in the region north of Metro Toronto said a patrolling officer spotted flames at the rear of an industrial area on the morning of September 1. Firefighters were called in and they made a grisly find: the body of a young girl had been stuffed inside a gasoline-soaked suitcase, wedged between two tires and set ablaze. Detailed forensic work revealed the girl was between eleven and seventeen years old, five-foot two, was dark-skinned and weighed between fifty and eighty pounds. She was originally from Ethiopia, the Sudan, Somalia or Egypt.

Police could find no missing persons reports for such a person and were unable to find a cause of death.

BIRKS HEIST FOILED

Toronto—September 1994

Metropolitan Toronto got a sharp taste of things to come when an Eastern European robbery team raided Birks, an upscale jewelry store in the downtown Eaton Centre in September 1994.

With the brazenness that typifies the single-minded violence of gangs out of the former Soviet Union, Edward Kotapski, a sixty-year-old parolee, and his partner, Dimitrios Batzakis, twenty-five, stormed into the elegant shop on the morning of December 17, 1993. Both men wore trench coats and had clear plastic masks over their faces. Kotapski was wielding a sawed-off shotgun. They forced a twenty-one-year-old clerk to open a display case, then began stuffing jewelry into pillowcases. A shot was fired into the ceiling of the store, alerting passersby, who called police.

Holdup squad detective Rick Huffman and Sergeant Brian Burger were in the area and they ran towards the shopping mall. Kotapski spotted the officers and took the clerk hostage, dragging her through the mall using her as a shield. Both robbers got to a parking garage, firing a shot at the officers as they dragged their hostage. Inside the garage, they let the clerk go and fled on foot. Batzakis was tackled nearby and police seized a handgun and $3 million worth of jewelry. Kotapski was later arrested in Montreal.

Justice Hugh Locke, noting Kotapski was on parole for armed robbery at the time of the Birks heist, sentenced him to fifteen years in prison. He called the Montreal man "a danger and a menace to society."

Batzakis was also called a danger to society and sentenced to nine years.

Kotapski is under investigation for several high-dollar robberies in Montreal and Toronto, including one in which an armored car guard was killed, and another Birks stickup.

DRINKING TO FORGET

Toronto—September 1994

A man who pleaded guilty to a savage assault on a stranger was acquitted anyway after a judge found his actions were "probably not voluntary" because he was too drunk.

Rayburn Misquadis, of Toronto, admitted attacking Thomas Curtis, fifty-seven, on February 11, 1994, after an evening of drinking.

Curtis had to use a cane for a month after being beaten by Misquadis at a downtown warehouse building.

In September 1994 Misquadis pleaded guilty to assault causing bodily harm and was remanded for sentencing.

But the same month the Supreme Court of Canada released a ruling in another case involving the defense of extreme drunkenness. When Misquadis appeared for sentencing, Judge Sam Darragh struck down his guilty plea, noting the attack was "probably not voluntary, and he probably lacked the capacity to form even the minimal intent required for the general-intent offense of assault causing bodily harm."

Curtis was angered at the ruling: "There is no justice left in this country. Now drunkenness will make law-breaking wide open. Get drunk out of your mind and you do anything you want."

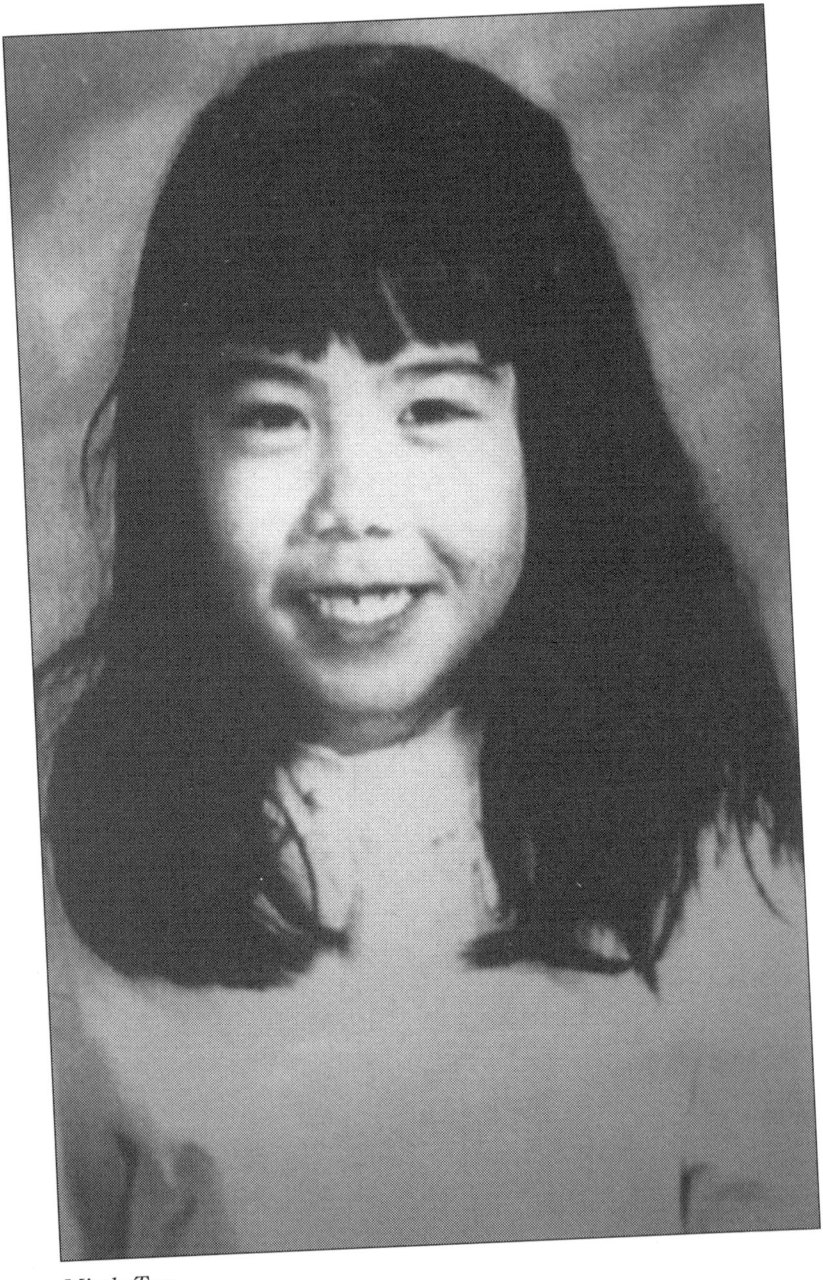

Mindy Tran

THE DEATH OF MINDY

LIKE SOME KIND of shrine to victims who fell in an incomprehensible war, the flowers and potted plants and stuffed animals were piled and stacked and lovingly placed at the edge of Mission Creek Park.

It is a scene that has become depressingly familiar in communities across Canada. At rape-murders, at fatal shooting scenes, at mysterious disappearances, at fatal car crashes. Bright flowers, cards of grief and hope, stuffed teddy bears.

In October 1994 the shrine was for Mindy Tran, an eight-year-old girl from Kelowna, British Columbia, whose path crossed with society's newest plague, the deranged sexual predator.

Before Mindy went missing on August 17, 1993, there were four members of the immediate Tran family, parents Johnny and Annie and daughters Mindy, eight, and Mimi, eighteen. The parents had come to Canada from Vietnam in 1979, at their backs a war-torn country, in front of them a new life of safety, peace and prosperity.

Johnny was a warehouse foreman, Annie a seamstress. The family lived in Rutland, a quiet suburb of Kelowna, in a well-kept home and were known as friendly and hardworking. A grade two student at Spring Valley elementary school, Mindy read a hundred books in her first year at school, two hundred and forty in her second. She enjoyed art, swimming, making cookies with her mother. Neighbors remember the young girl as staying close to the family home, seldom riding her bike more than seven or eight houses away.

The last time anyone saw Mindy Tran alive was at seven o'clock on August 17. She was riding her bicycle near her home on the quiet summer evening. Then she was gone.

A massive campaign involving hundreds of residents and teams of police officers went into gear. Posters were passed out, media appeals were broadcast, searches were organized. A police hot line was set up. Kelowna was galvanized into action: the hot line quickly netted five thousand calls.

Parks, backyards, garages, abandoned buildings, even sewers were searched. The area was gridded into search zones.

Among the searchers was a forty-four-year-old transient, a boarder who lived in the basement of a duplex on Taylor Road near Mindy's home. The man, an auto mechanic and ex-convict, had been convicted of robbery in 1987 in Newfoundland and had once been sentenced to nine months for assault causing bodily harm. There were no sexual offenses on his record. He'd lived in the area for five months and he quickly went onto the list of suspects in the disappearance.

Investigators interviewed the man and checked his alibi. Superficially, it held, corroborated by his friends. Teams of detectives continued probing the mysterious disappearance. Within days it became apparent the searchers weren't looking for a lost child. They were looking for a body.

Police from seven area jurisdictions met to look for common links between the Mindy Tran case and several unsolved disappearances and murders of children and young women.

On October 11, two months after Mindy went missing, searchers acting on a tip from a Vancouver-area psychic went to Mission Creek Park. Concentrating on a wooded area that had been searched half a dozen times, they were alerted by a strong odor coming from the base of a towering tree. One searcher poked at a pile of leaves and spotted a running shoe. It belonged to Mindy Tran. The little girl's body was in a hollow, carefully covered with dirt, leaves and branches.

Dental records were used to positively identify the remains. An autopsy showed she'd been sexually attacked and strangled.

As the murder probe kicked into high gear with twenty-six Mounties assigned to the case, police put the ex-convict auto mechanic at the top of their suspect list and the Tran family planned a public funeral for their daughter.

A shrine of flowers and plants and stuffed animals sprung up almost overnight. The town was rocked by grief and anger. Parents kept a close eye on their children, and anyone acting suspiciously was reported to police. One man, spotted hugging a young boy, was investigated: he was merely breaking up a fight among neighborhood children. Police responded to several similar reports.

On Wednesday, October 19, thousands turned out to lay Mindy Tran to rest. The chapel of the Springfield funeral home was crowded and a public address system was set up outside for mourners who couldn't get in.

A poem was read as Mindy lay in a small oak casket, flanked by a candle and wreaths of yellow flowers. "It broke our hearts to lose you, Though you didn't go alone; For part of us went with you, The day God took you home." Reverend Albert Baldeo spoke of his "sense of helplessness" as he stood before the casket, of "a violent attack on helplessness, a violent attack on childhood." A choir from Mindy's school sang her favorite song, "A Whole New World," from the movie *Aladdin*.

She was buried at the city cemetery.

The murder investigation forged ahead. A homicide task force looked at every aspect of the mechanic's life and picked apart his initial alibi. Inconsistencies began to emerge—the timing was off and the whole story was going sideways on the suspect.

Police found it was hard to keep secret the identity of their prime suspect. On January 5, 1995, three friends of the man learned he was the main suspect in the investigation. They confronted him at the park where Mindy had been found dead and tried to beat a confession out of him. He pulled a gun and pointed it. They disarmed him and beat him to within an inch of his life. He was hospitalized for eleven days.

The police hoped to keep a lid on the beating, fearing the investigation could be jeopardized. But the three vigilantes called local media outlets and bragged of the beating. RCMP contacted each media outlet and gained their cooperation. When the man was released from hospital he was charged with four weapons offenses. Two days later, he pleaded guilty to two charges and was sent to jail for two years. The prison put him into segregation when, inevitably, his link to the Mindy murder became known.

The arrest and conviction gave police some much-needed breathing space. Their suspect was on ice. Detailed forensic evidence, including DNA tests, were under way. "We're in no hurry.

The individual is in jail and he'll be there for two years. We're not being pressured into anything. There's not a risk to society right now as far as that individual is concerned," RCMP Sergeant Peter Montague told the *Vancouver Sun*.

Edmonton police revealed they'd spent the past four months looking at the Tran case and at the suspect for links to the September 1992 abduction, sexual assault and murder of a six-year-old girl. They said the suspect had been living in Edmonton at the time the girl was slain.

At the beginning of February, even though RCMP in Kelowna had laid no charge in the Tran case, Superintendent Rod MacKay held a press conference and, in a bid to reassure and calm the city's citizens, revealed they were pretty sure who the killer was. He said the case had been submitted to the Crown. "We're alerting the public that our prime suspect is in custody at this time," MacKay said.

As this book goes to press, RCMP are continuing to conduct forensic tests in the Tran case. The Edmonton murder hasn't yet resulted in charges.

DNA PROOF LEADS TO GUILTY PLEA

Surrey—October 1994

Paroled rapist Mitchell James Owen quickly changed his plea to guilty when a DNA report linked him to blood found in the mouth of a murdered sixteen-year-old woman.

Pamela Cameron

Pamela Cameron, formerly of Burlington, Ontario, was found strangled to death on October 4, 1994, in a wooded area of Surrey, near Vancouver. The teen, whose family had recently moved from Milton, near Toronto, to the West Coast, had been raped.

Owen, thirty-nine, had twenty-eight previous criminal convictions, including several for weapons offenses and one for rape. He had served most of a ten-year sentence for raping and robbing a Vancouver woman in 1982. At his trial for that attack, Judge Ross Collver called him "a walking time bomb."

In prison Owen refused to undergo treatment for his sexual behavior and wouldn't participate in a program to treat substance abuse.

He was released on statutory supervision, twice violated his parole conditions and had time added to his sentence. Corrections Canada labeled him a high-risk inmate when he was released in 1992.

After his release he went to the Metro Toronto area where detectives kept him under close watch. On March 6, 1994, when his sentence expired, Owen was able to leave Toronto, and in July he headed to British Columbia. Because he wasn't required to report his movements or activities to police any longer, RCMP in British Columbia had no idea he was in their jurisdiction.

On October 4, 1994, Owen jumped Pamela Cameron as she walked along 152nd Street in Surrey, British Columbia, on her way to visit her boyfriend. She was dragged into a wooded area where she was attacked.

Cameron bravely fought her assailant and bit into his fingers as he ripped off her clothes and strangled her to death. His blood was in her mouth when her body was discovered hidden under a pile of leaves the following day.

Twelve days later Owen, exhausted by running from a massive police manhunt, turned himself in to Vancouver police. He was still bleeding from bite wounds. At Owen's brother's home police seized discarded bloody bandages. There was also blood on a bag Owen owned.

Samples of all the blood was sent for DNA testing and a match was made indicating it was his blood in her mouth.

After results were released to Owen's lawyer, the accused man changed his plea to guilty. He was sentenced to life in prison with no parole for twenty-five years, although he could apply after fifteen.

But the sentencing didn't mean the end of the story for the Cameron family. Pamela's parents, Marilyn and Paul, vow to campaign for tougher penalties for violent offenders: "My campaign is going to get stronger now," Marilyn Cameron said after Owen was sentenced. "I just know that my daughter did not die in vain."

NOTORIOUS CRIMINAL CAUGHT

Port Perry—October 1994

One of Canada's most notorious criminals was arrested in October 1994 after a botched bank heist in the quiet community of Port Perry, east of Metro Toronto.

Mitchell (Mickey) McArthur, lifetime crook and author of *I'd Rather Be Wanted Than Had—The Memoirs of an Unrepentant Bank Robber*, was arrested along with his brother Angus after a pair of bandits shot five people, including three police officers, in a bloody raid on a Bank of Montreal branch.

Witnesses told police the gunmen, wearing balaclavas and long overcoats, went into the bank at 7:27 p.m. on Thursday, October 21, and herded eight employees and customers to the back of the room before making their way to the vault. Bank manager Alan Knight, forty-five, was shot in the leg when he refused to give up the combination to the vault. The robbers scooped up cash in two white sacks and fled the building.

As police began arriving, the bandits, who were fleeing on bicycles, opened fire. Constable Mark McConkey, forty-five, had his jaw shattered by a bullet; fragments hit Constable Warren Ellis, twenty-eight, and lodged between his brain and skull. Detective Paul Mooy, forty-five, jumped from his car and fired a shot before being hit in the arm. Another round, apparently a stray, pierced the window of a real estate office two hundred meters away and hit Debbie Taylor, forty-one, in the chest.

The gunmen escaped and kidnapped Harry Pearce, seventy-four, from the driveway of his nearby home. They drove off in his van to the parking lot of Port Perry Hospital, where they released the elderly man unharmed before jumping into a red Camaro and speeding away.

A massive manhunt began, involving dozens of police and a helicopter equipped with an infrared heat-seeking device. Early the next morning, investigators tracked two suspects to homes in the Kingston area. Heavily armed tactical officers, including sharpshooters, raided the homes and arrested McArthur and his brother. Both face numerous charges, including several of attempted murder. Charged with obstruction in the case was one Margaret Wilkinson.

All five shooting victims recovered, or are recovering, from their wounds.

The robbery case led to the reexamination of a twelve-year-old mystery that has baffled police for twelve years. In November 1982 Tom Gencarelli vanished after leaving his Kingston apartment to go to work. Detectives were puzzled at the disappearance and suspected foul play. Gencarelli's wife, pregnant at the time, was the same Margaret Wilkinson charged with the McArthurs. In November, after Wilkinson's arrest, police and Canadian Forces teams resumed their search for Gencarelli.

TEENS GET TEN FOR MURDER

Saskatoon—October 1994

Two teens who stabbed and beat to death a Saskatoon-area farmer were sent to prison for ten years in October 1994.

Ricky Jay Tourangeau was fifteen at the time of the murder; Edward Cote was seventeen. The pair were two of five young men charged and convicted in the September 1992 slaying of John Chester Sorgenson, of Kamsack, Saskatchewan.

Sorgenson, forty-one, was a truly innocent victim of random deadly violence. He was a three-hundred-pound working man—called "the old man" or "a teddy bear"—who was easygoing and never got caught up in the racial tensions that sometimes divide parts of the Saskatchewan community. He was known as a man who got along well with all cultural groups.

Not wealthy by any means, Sorgenson lived in a small bungalow. Riches weren't very high on his list of priorities. "He did a lot of work for next to nothing or didn't charge very much," his eighty-year-old father, Chester, remembered in an interview with the *Saskatoon Star Phoenix*.

John Chester, who never married, worked in the construction trade until his foot was crushed in the late 1980s. Unable to continue in the business, he did small welding jobs.

When someone had trouble, residents said, Sorgenson was the first to drop whatever he was doing and go to their aid.

And it was that good-natured sense of community that led to his death.

On September 4, 1992, six young people, Ricky and Lazy Joe Tourangeau, Christopher and Charles Gordon, Charles's common-law wife, Sharon Tourangeau, and Edward Cote, were in an old Dodge Monaco, cruising around the Cote reserve. Charles was driving the car; the group had just picked up five dozen beers, and, as Sharon later testified, they were looking for trouble.

First they drove north and stopped at a farm. Sharon said she and Charles waited in the car while the others went into the yard looking for gas.

It was four in the morning when Peter Belley, seventy-seven, was awakened by his small dog. "I opened the door just a little way and then I noticed the outside door was open. I reached out to close it and got hit in the face, in my eye and nose. I thought somebody had shot me."

Reeling from the blow from a tire iron, Belley staggered back and kicked the door shut, yelling to his wife to put on the lights and call the police. He grabbed his .303 rifle and guarded the hallway, waiting for police.

Scared off by the confrontation with the old man, the attackers returned to the Dodge. Chris Gordon said he'd hit a man. The group drove up the road to Sorgenson's home.

Gordon and Ricky Tourangeau went to the door and awakened Sorgenson, saying they needed a boost for the Dodge. Obligingly, Sorgenson came out and moved his pickup into position to boost the car.

And they began killing him. They beat him with tire irons and stabbed him repeatedly. They left him for dead in a clump of bushes, his head battered in and nine knife wounds in his back. The gang broke into his house, making off with several hundred dollars. Before fleeing, they set Sorgenson's pickup on fire.

Sharon Tourangeau testified that after the slaying she threw a knife into Stoney Creek on the Key reserve. She said someone else tossed another knife and a tire iron from a bridge into a river.

They stopped to buy a wreck for $250, then went on a beer run, running up a total of $165. Later they split up and went home.

Early on September 4 RCMP Constable Lloyd Yew was called to Belley's home. He took the report and was headed to Kamsack when he got a call to go to Sorgenson's home, where a pickup was burning. After firefighters doused the truck, Yew looked around and found Sorgenson's body covered in blood.

Early on February 5, RCMP Corporal Tim Baulkham found Chris Gordon drunk in a ditch on the Key reserve. He took him to Kamsack. There Baulkham met Ricky Jay and Lazy Joe Tourangeau, who had surrendered. Within the next two hours the corporal picked up Charles Gordon and Cote.

In 1993 Christopher Gordon was convicted of first-degree murder and sentenced to life without parole for twenty-five years. His brother, Charles, and Lazy Joe Tourangeau were found guilty of second-degree murder.

Because of their ages, the younger Tourangeau and Edward Cote were the subjects of a special application to elevate their cases to adult court. They were tried as adults, and in the autumn of 1994 both were convicted of second-degree murder. They will be eligible for parole in five or ten years.

Some appeals have been filed.

Though the five suspects were convicted, Sorgenson's parents still have trouble dealing with their bachelor son's death. His mother, Mary, can't discuss it at all. Chester Sorgenson remembers a patient, kind son who never had a bad word for anyone.

"This should never, ever happen to anyone, to any family," Chester says. "It's the most senseless thing that I ever heard of."

CONVICTED KILLER ESCAPES

Barrie—October 1994

A convicted killer who escaped prison to highlight his bid for a new trial wound up back in custody. But the high profile given Allan Kinsella's escape is expected to lead to a reexamination of his case.

Kinsella, fifty-three, was convicted with Ted Sale in the 1978 slaying of motel clerk Ken Kaplinski, who was shot dead during a robbery in Barrie, Ontario. Kinsella and Sale were found guilty of first-degree murder and sentenced to life in prison with no parole.

Throughout the trial and his subsequent sixteen years in prison, Kinsella maintained he wasn't involved in the murder of Kaplinski. He said he was asleep during the slaying.

In October 1994 Kinsella and another inmate escaped from the Bath Institution near Kingston. Kinsella was captured two weeks later by police in Toronto. The other man—also a convicted killer—was caught by U.S. authorities as he tried to cross the border.

Kinsella's escape led Justice Minister Allan Rock to ask for all materials pertaining to the case, including a statement in which Ted Sale said Kinsella was drunk and unconscious in their car while he, Sale, shot Kaplinski. Sale swore that the botched robbery was planned and carried out without Kinsella's assistance.

The case remains under review.

A LOW-LIFE TALE

Saskatoon—October 1994

The Ronald Anderson–Seline Bahsler story was a low-life tale of two of society's losers. One lost a piece of his life and the other lost hers entirely.

Seline Bahsler was forty-two years old when her body was found under a rusted abandoned bus in the backyard of a rundown house in Saskatoon in October 1993. Her body was battered and bruised; she had been strangled.

Bahsler, who had two teenaged children, was a shy but happy

person with few interests. She lived her life among towering shadows of abuse: drugs and booze and strange men. She moved in a circle of people down on their luck who never quite fit themselves into the mainstream life. She often floated into treatment programs for her excesses and visited Alcoholics Anonymous several times.

Ronald Anderson, too, saw life through altered vision. The forty-four-year-old former heroin addict had fled home at the age of twelve, leaving behind an abusive stepfather. He had racked up thirty-one criminal convictions throughout the West but still, intermittently, managed a successful life for himself, holding down responsible jobs and doing work for Narcotics Anonymous, a group that had helped him through his own struggles.

But the violence of his childhood and his inability to deal with it regularly nudged him over the edge, back into a free-falling world of substance abuse.

In 1992 both Bahsler and Anderson were in critical down phases of their lives and it seemed unsurprising, if not somehow mandated, that they'd meet as they moved through the world of self-abuse and Saskatoon watering holes.

And by October 1993 their paths had crossed a few times, intersecting lines of sex and booze. On the fateful night, the couple were together in Anderson's basement apartment after drinking at a local bar.

Anderson's account of what happened in his room was spotted by blackouts and dim recollections. He said the couple had sex and at one point he snapped out of a black spell and found himself having anal sex with Bahsler.

He said he felt disgusted and went to the washroom to clean up. "When I came back she wanted more to drink and I had nothing to drink," he testified. When he told Bahsler to leave, she threatened to charge him with rape. "I grabbed her by the throat and told her to get her clothes on," he said.

As he forced her out of the house in a hammerlock, he pulled a shirt over her head so she wouldn't see the house number. Bahsler fought back, kicking and punching and scratching, he said. "I lost it. I think I punched her twice in the head. I saw red; I flipped out."

Another blackout rolled in and he found himself on top of the woman near an abandoned bus. "She was on her back...her eyes were closed and it was like she was exhaling except there was a gurgling sound to it. The street expression for it is a death rattle."

He was arrested a short time later and charged with second-degree murder. He testified he thought he was defending himself, not committing an assault.

Prepared to plead guilty to manslaughter, Anderson was surprised that the Crown took him to trial on the murder charge.

One year after the killing, in October 1994, the jury brought in a guilty verdict, rejecting his claim that he was undergoing an anxiety attack at the time of the slaying and had no intent to kill.

Anderson was sentenced to life in prison. Justice I. K. McLellan said he must serve ten years—the minimum—before being eligible for parole.

Justice McLellan wrapped up the entire chain of events when he said: "Both [Anderson and Bahsler] were unfortunate members of society suffering from severe alcohol dependency."

ASSAULT ON ABORTION DOCTOR

Vancouver—November 1994

Dr. Garson Romalis was having breakfast at his Vancouver home on the morning of November 8, 1994, when a sniper opened fire with an assault rifle.

Romalis, whose home had in the past been picketed by anti-abortion demonstrators, was hit in the leg. The bullet, believed to have been fired from an AK-47 assault rifle, severed a major artery, causing heavy bleeding. Romalis treated himself and called emergency services. After undergoing treatment at a local hospital, he was listed in serious but stable condition.

Detectives said Romalis, a gynecologist and obstetrician who works at the Women's Health Centre and the Elizabeth Bagshaw clinic in Vancouver, was the target of a murder attempt. They immediately set up a task force and centered their probe on the antiabortion movement, but admitted they had no motive in the shooting.

Antiabortionists condemned the shooting and reacted negatively when the provincial government set up a new police unit to probe violence against doctors and patients involved in abortions.

Attorney General Colin Gablemann said doctors and patients must be free of intimidation, and he vowed that the government would use the full force of the law to make sure that happens.

Detectives are tracking people who bought the rare cartridge used in the shooting.

BUDREO: A LEGAL DILEMMA

Peterborough—November 1994

The rights of the individual and the rights of society came into conflict with the twisting case of convicted pedophile Wray Budreo.

Budreo, a homosexual pedophile with twenty-two convictions, was released from prison in November 1994 after serving every

A CRIMINAL HAVEN

In November 1994 a prominent Italian jurist told a global crime symposium in Toronto that Canada is becoming a haven for organized crime.

Nicola Gratteri, a top anti-Mafia prosecutor, speaking at York University, said at least ten criminal syndicates, including Italian, Russian, Colombian and Chinese, are operating in Canada because of lenient immigration laws, lax financial restrictions and a lenient judicial system.

Gratteri urged Canada to bring in anti-Mafia legislation, warning: "This battle is too large to be waged by any single country…it must be fought by the world community."

Journalist and author Antonio Nicaso said criminal summit meetings are being held in Canada and added that current money-laundering laws are satisfactory to no one "except the banks and the criminals."

possible moment of a six-year sentence for sexual assault on three boys in Brampton, west of Metro Toronto.

Budreo, who took treatment in prison and continued psychiatric counseling upon release, was "chemically castrated" with medication.

After his release, the fifty-year-old ex-convict went to Peterborough where he stayed with a sponsor. But the city's police chief, Kevin McAlpine, warned residents to be cautious of the high-risk repeat offender. Police said the warning was issued because the public's safety outweighed Budreo's privacy.

Budreo went on CHEX-TV and tried to fight the media frenzy his release sparked. Saying he's "not a monster" but a man trying to get on with his life, Budreo pleaded for understanding: "I believe I can [live a normal life] if I'm given a chance."

On November 20 Budreo traveled to Toronto where he contacted police and met with them. Spokesman Louise Gray said he cooperated with detectives and let them know where he was staying. At a Toronto hospital he was given an injection to reduce his sex drive.

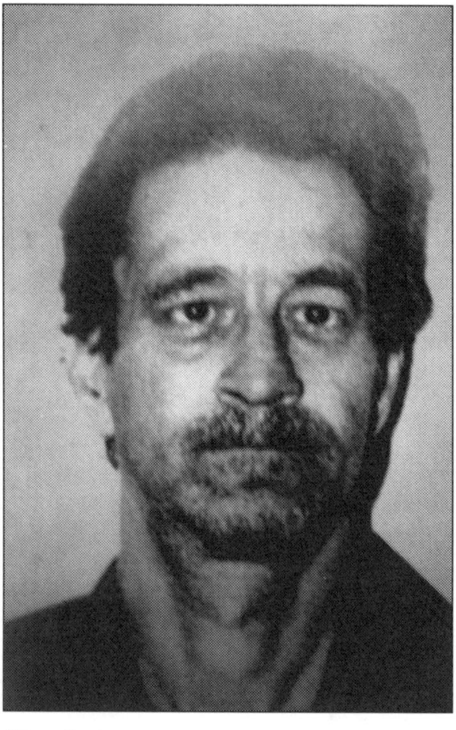

Wray Budreo

Two days later he was arrested by Metro officers because they feared he would reoffend. Police applied to court under a 1993 law to have him placed on a peace bond to restrict his access to children.

The arrest sparked a constitutional challenge, pitting civil liberties against victims' rights. The issue hasn't been resolved.

THE CASE OF THE SPIKED GRAVY

Halifax—November 1994

In late November 1994 a Nova Scotia court handed Laura Lillian Dengenhardt an automatic life sentence in the murder of her husband, Frederick.

Frederick, 59, was killed in October 1993 after his wife spiked his gravy with drugs so she could have sex with her boyfriend, David Murray Brown. Laura Dengenhardt, 48, and Brown, 26, had been lovers since early 1993, court was told.

A few hours before the October 28 murder Laura put drugs in her husband's gravy. Brown took the victim to a nearby bridge, picked him up by the heels and dropped him into the Herbert River.

After her husband's death, Laura faked a suicide attempt, taping a final message on a karaoke machine to make it appear she couldn't deal with the loss of her husband.

An autopsy showed Frederick Dengenhardt died of "dry drowning," a condition caused when cold water constricts the throat muscles, resulting in suffocation of the victim without any water entering the lungs. The autopsy also revealed high levels of a sedative Laura had a prescription for.

Two months later police arrested the widow and her lover. Both were charged with murder.

At his trial in November 1994 Brown wept as he was sent to prison for life, without the possibility of parole for twenty-five years. He said he had been following Laura's instructions.

A week after Brown's sentencing, Laura was also given an automatic life term. She won't be eligible for parole for fifteen years.

BAD BLOOD

Moser River—November 1994

Bad blood between two families in a remote village on Nova Scotia's eastern shore ended with a prisoner dead in a local jail.

Donald Findlay, thirty-seven, was beaten to death while

serving time at the Halifax County Correctional Centre. He was attacked on October 1, 1993, the court was told.

Findlay, a muscular excavating contractor serving time for ramming his truck into a car driven by men he believed had threatened his son, was attacked as other prisoners watched. His attacker, Wade Gerald Fleet, repeatedly stomped and punched Findlay in the head and neck as he lay on his cot, the Nova Scotia Supreme Court jury heard.

The court was told of a longtime ongoing feud between the Findlays and the Fleets in Moser River. Several residents had complained of a lawless bunch of people who terrorized the town for years. Donald Findlay, they said, stood up to them.

When Findlay arrived at the Halifax CCC to begin serving a two-weekend intermittent sentence for dangerous driving, Fleet attacked him. The prosecution said Fleet hated Findlay and had planned to attack him on his arrival.

On December 6, 1994, the jury returned after twelve hours of deliberation. They found Fleet guilty of first-degree murder.

Fleet stood quietly as the verdict was read. His family sobbed behind him. When asked if he had anything to say, he said "No." He received an automatic life sentence without parole for twenty-five years. But under recent changes, a prisoner can apply for a judicial review after fifteen years.

Donald Findlay's widow, Dorothy, said she was "pleased" with the verdict. She said she has no intention of leaving Moser River, despite the feud. "I hope it sends a message to the people in Moser River to speak out and let them know that it does work: to holler and scream and jump up and down."

Fleet's lawyer said he plans to appeal the case.

HATE STATS

Metropolitan Toronto police recorded 249 complaints of hate-motivated crimes in 1994—a sixty-one percent jump over the previous year.

Eighty-eight of the crimes involved assault, generally unprovoked and random. The city's black and Jewish communities were usually the targets of the attacks.

Detective-Sergeant Wayne Cotgreave, of the force's hate crimes unit, said the figures reflect an increase in community awareness. Arrests of suspects are up sharply, from thirty-one in 1993 to ninety in 1994.

Most disturbing, Cotgreave said, is the large number of young people charged in hate crimes, sixty-one out of the ninety arrests.

Julie Stanton

WHERE'S JULIE?

IN DECEMBER 1994, police in Durham Region, east of Metro Toronto, got a conviction in the most difficult of cases: the nobody homicide.

Peter John Stark, forty-nine, was sentenced to a life term after being convicted in the slaying of Julie Anne Stanton. The fourteen-year-old had disappeared April 16, 1990, Easter Monday, after leaving her Pickering home. She was never seen again.

Massive searches by police and volunteers failed to find any sign of the pretty blond teen. While the searches went on, Durham detectives targeted Peter Stark, the father of one of Julie's friends, as a suspect in the case.

Stark was a natural for investigation. His name came up on a list of suspects in the disappearance of his friend Marie Woods, who vanished in 1981. Her remains were found five years later in the bush north of Toronto. And Stark had previously served six years in prison for a frenzied stabbing attack on a female hitchhiker.

In an interview, Stark admitted the stabbing attack, saying he "went crazy" and couldn't remember what happened. He referred to a car accident that caused him brain damage.

Stark's history with Julie Anne Stanton came to light during the probe into her disappearance. In July 1989 he'd lured her to his boat, *Polara II*, at the Darlington Marina, where he drugged her with Halcion; there were reports of another similar incident between Stark and Stanton.

Durham Region detectives quickly determined that Stark was their best suspect. They conducted hundreds of interviews to tie Stark to the missing teen on the day of the disappearance.

They found Stark had called Stanton on Easter Monday when she was alone at home. Stark made arrangements with the teen and picked her up at two that afternoon in his gray 1979 Chevy Monte Carlo. Witnesses remembered the car as needing a new muffler.

Teams of detectives went after Stark. They searched his boat, seized his car and interviewed anyone who could possibly have information on the case. Stark's wife, Alison, turned against him and cooperated with police. In a conversation secretly recorded by the police, she told officers she'd seen eight fingernail scratches on her husband the night Stanton disappeared. Alison said she confronted her husband. According to Alison, Stark replied, "I did not pick that fucking kid up. I did not fucking kill anybody." He also expressed frustration with being under investigation: "Fine...let them arrest me....Let's get this shit over with."

A month later, on February 11, 1992, almost two years after the disappearance, detectives took Stark's advice and charged him with first-degree murder.

During Stark's trial, Crown attorney John Scott led a series of witnesses who built a circumstantial case around the accused. Reporters, friends, relatives, Alison Stark and a hardened criminal were among those who testified.

Police believe Stark took Stanton to an unknown location where he drugged, raped and murdered her. How he disposed of the body isn't known, but in an alleged jailhouse confession after he was arrested, he reportedly told Gerald Udall, another prisoner: "Between you and me, Gerald, yeah." Udall said Stark told him Stanton was drugged with sleeping pills, then raped.

Udall, who said Stark showed no remorse, testified: "It was like staring into no eyes. [He had] no feelings and was very cold. He wanted to [have sex with] her, but she wouldn't go for it. Then he got scared she was going to run to her parents. That's when he chopped her up with an ax."

Stark's lawyer, Leo Adler, called no evidence, and the jury took just seven hours to bring in a guilty verdict. Adler said after the trial he intended to appeal the case.

But even with the conviction, police admit the case isn't over. "We're not giving up....The case won't be closed until we find Julie's remains," Detective Harold Curwain said.

And for the Stanton family, until they have a body to bury, it will never end. After Stark's conviction, John Stanton asked the convicted man: "Where's Julie, Peter?"

DISABILITY AND DEATH

Hamilton—December 1994

Cathie Wilkieson loved her son, Ryan.

On Monday, December 5, 1994, she put the sixteen-year-old, who suffered from cerebral palsy and was deaf and blind, into the backseat of the family station wagon, which was parked in the garage of their Hamilton, Ontario, home. She climbed in and turned on the engine. Both died of carbon monoxide poisoning. She was found sitting in the backseat of the car, holding Ryan cradled in her arms with a blanket over him.

A suicide note Cathie Wilkieson wrote said she just wanted to go to sleep and didn't want to leave Ryan alone.

What should have been a deep family tragedy quickly became a lightning rod for the rights of the disabled and their families.

Members of Family Alliance, a lobby group for the disabled, said the deaths were sparked by despair over funding for the disabled. There were reports that Cathie Wilkieson was devastated when her request for eleven more hours of help a week was turned down.

The allegation spurred the Ontario government, which spends more than $1 billion annually in cash and services to help the disabled, to vow to push forward new policies.

An inquest into the murder-suicide was held in the spring of 1995. Wilkieson's husband, Neil, lashed out at Family Alliance for "making our pain and grief so much harder to bear."

He had harsh words for the group: "They're the most disgusting group I've ever met." He said statements about his wife being turned down for extra funding were "outright lies." The deaths, he added, were a personal matter and had nothing to do with lack of funding.

And he praised government and school services: "I believe Cathie was taken advantage of and manipulated at a time when she was depressed. They [government services] were more than helpful."

The inquest jury admitted they didn't fully understand the deaths, but they didn't agree that the tragedy was related to funding. Among the jurors' recommendations was that advocacy groups establish guidelines regarding the use of personal and private information.

The case echoed the circumstances of Saskatchewan farmer Robert Latimer and his twelve-year-old daughter, Tracy, who suffered from severe cerebral palsy. The child was in constant pain, had to wear diapers and weighed only seventeen kilograms. She couldn't talk, walk or feed herself.

On October 14, 1993, Latimer, forty-one, vented exhaust fumes into his truck to kill her. He confessed to the slaying. In November 1994 he was convicted of murder and sentenced to life in prison without eligibility for parole for ten years. The sentence is the minimum available for second-degree murder.

Latimer is appealing the verdict and the sentence.

MYSTERY DEATH

Toronto—December 1994

Prominent criminal lawyer Eddie Greenspan slammed Metro Toronto homicide detectives for treating the distraught parents of a dead nine-year-old girl as suspects.

Audrey Cohen, a physically and mentally disabled Scarborough girl, died after she collapsed in the family home on Boxing Day, 1994. Emergency personnel called the police, and the homicide squad was sent to the family's home.

Homicide detectives said they were unable to interview the parents, but spoke to their lawyer. Detective Peter Gibson wouldn't reveal why the homicide squad was called in.

After news reports circulated that neither Paul nor Elspeth Cohen was refusing to cooperate in the investigation, lawyer Greenspan put out a press release chastising police for treating them as suspects.

Greenspan, one of the foremost criminal lawyers in Canada, said police didn't see the Cohens as "parents devastated by tragedy but rather as suspects in some type of crime."

He wrote: "The police were not prepared to treat this family as a family in mourning and in a state of shock." He added that his clients' refusal to speak to police was "totally understandable."

After Greenspan's news release, detectives were loath to comment on the case. In early summer, the homicide squad announced no charges will be laid. An inquest will be held into the girl's death.

CRIME RATE STABLE

Random violence was blamed for Canadians' misperception of the amount of crime in the country, a federally funded study reported at the end of December 1994.

Sponsored by the federal Justice Department and run by a criminologist at the University of Ottawa, the study compared opinion polls with trends in crimes and victimization surveys.

Public Knowledge of Crime and Justice: An Inventory of Canadian Findings showed although two-thirds of Canadians believe crime has risen during the previous five years, statistics indicate the crime rate has remained generally stable.

The report showed most Canadians believe homicides are increasing more than other crimes. But the numbers showed homicides have either remained stable or have decreased.

A review of gun crimes showed 37% of robberies in 1978 involved a gun; by 1990 the number had fallen to 26%. Homicides involving guns rose slightly, from 32% in 1980 to 34% in 1992.

On the justice front, the report showed Canadians believe the parole system is lax and that more than half of prisoners get parole. In fact, only 34% of prisoners gain parole, a number virtually unchanged for the past ten years. Between 1978 and 1988 almost 75% of parolees completed their sentences successfully. And only 12% had their paroles revoked for reoffending.

STALKER PAYS UP

Ottawa—December 1994

An Ottawa man who stalked and threatened his wife—even climbing a tree to videotape her through her bathroom window—was ordered to pay her $105,000.

Anthony Buelow, fifty-four, took away the thirty-one-year-old woman's enjoyment of life and put her through four months of mental, physical and emotional anguish, Mr. Justice Kenneth Binks ruled. "At the recommendation of her family doctor and the police, [she has] assumed a new name and relocated with her daughter to a new community."

Binks said the victim's health went to hell: she suffered severe depression, short-term memory loss, insomnia, loss of appetite, weight loss, eczema and loss of self-esteem.

The court was told Buelow threatened to kidnap the woman's daughter. He also told people he had nude movies of her, taken when he climbed up a tree and videotaped her in her bathroom.

"There's no way you can get away from me," he told her.

Melanie Carpenter

Fernand Auger

THE DEATH OF MELANIE CARPENTER

SEX OFFENDER Fernand Emond Auger was on statutory release in January 1995. The thirty-seven-year-old psychopath had served sixteen months of a two-year sentence for robbing a Calgary gas station. His criminal record included convictions in Toronto for sexually attacking and buggering juvenile prostitutes. He was sentenced to two years. Then he turned up out West, where he was charged and convicted in the gas station robbery. In November 1993, he applied for parole but was turned down because he was considered a risk to reoffend. In August 1994, having served two-thirds of his robbery sentence, Auger was freed from Bowden Institution, near Calgary.

Melanie Carpenter had five months to live.

Carpenter was twenty-three years old in January 1995. She had blond hair and brown eyes, and was attractive, friendly and intelligent.

On Friday, January 6, Carpenter was working alone as manager at Island Tan, a tanning salon in Surrey, British Columbia.

Two suspicious occurrences had already happened Friday morning. First, police received reports that a suspicious-looking man had been lurking around the salon. Second, police were told a man had called Carpenter and asked her to clear the salon of customers between one and two o'clock because a group of Japanese businessmen was coming through; they were interested in buying an Island Tan franchise. Carpenter had called her boss, who came to the salon to take a second call from the man. When the man refused to give his phone number, the incident was written off as a hoax.

In the afternoon a customer stopped in to make an appointment, then left. When the customer returned, the salon was empty. Cash was gone from the till, Carpenter's bag and jacket were in the salon, and her car was parked outside.

Tracing usage on her banking card, detectives found a withdrawal for $300 had been made the same afternoon in a shopping center. The surveillance camera at the ATM captured a photograph of the man who used it. On Saturday police released the dark, fuzzy photo of a man wearing sunglasses. The picture was enhanced and circulated throughout the area. Melanie's father, Steve, went on TV and made a public appeal for his daughter, waving a fistful of hundred-dollar bills, begging for her life.

The police probe quickly centered on Fernand Auger and a nationwide manhunt began. Police found no trace of him until January 15, when his body was found by a rental agent in a rented red Hyundai Excel in a garage near High River, Alberta, sixty kilometers south of Calgary. The garage was sealed, and Auger had used a hose to pipe carbon monoxide from the exhaust into the vehicle.

A search of his small one-bedroom apartment above a Chinese restaurant turned up a Bible, a self-help prison workbook and a copy of *Final Exit*, a how-to book on suicide. In the workbook, beside a question that asked the prisoner what he liked about himself, Auger had written: "Ability to help others." He described himself as "powerless" and "lost."

A brief suicide note dated January 9, three days after the abduction and written on a car-rental inspection report, said in part: "My death was chosen my way my choice my place and time." He made no reference to Carpenter or to what happened to her body. He made his goodbyes to family and friends.

Three weeks after Carpenter vanished, Art Tooke and Steve Emery were scavenging for old fishing nets near a sideroad off the TransCanada Highway about two hundred kilometers east of Vancouver. The men spotted a rolled-up blanket. "I lifted it up and I looked at it three or four seconds," Emery later told a reporter. "I [saw] blond hair and [a] face. I knew it was a body."

Melanie Carpenter was dead, stabbed more than twenty times and sexually attacked. Her hands were tightly bound behind her back. She'd apparently been killed within hours of her disappearance, and her body dumped in the rugged Fraser Canyon.

Steve Carpenter reacted with grief and anger, calling for tougher laws to control dangerous offenders. He went on *The Shirley Show* and made his point: "These people should be locked up for life. If we're going to make a mistake, let's make it on the side of safety."

In February, twenty-five hundred people marched in Surrey to demand tougher laws. Sandra Cunningham, who puts out a newsletter warning about child sex offenders free in the community, told politicians that their jobs were at stake. "Listen up. The decision you make in regards to this matter could very well be a career decision."

NEW YEAR'S SHOOTING RAMPAGE

Toronto—January 1995

A Metro Toronto man who rang in the New Year with gunfire—leaving two people wounded—was sent to prison for fourteen and a half years.

Roberto Camara, twenty-five, wore a semiautomatic pistol in a shoulder holster when he went to a New Year's party at Studio 69, a downtown nightclub.

When other partygoers complained Camara was spraying them with champagne, doorman Joe Palma took the bottle from the armed man. Camara pulled out his gun and shot Palma and another man in the legs. Palma, a former university basketball player and martial artist, had his kneecap blown off and was permanently disabled.

Joe Tassone, the bar's owner, confronted Camara; Camara grabbed Tassone and pointed the gun at his temple. Tassone was told: "Let's go. I'm going to blow your head off." Camara pulled the trigger twice but the gun was empty.

Mr. Justice George Ferguson described the violence as "unprovoked." He said Camara was a man with "a history of violence and a total disregard for court orders, prohibitions and the lives of others."

As Camara was led from the courtroom in handcuffs, he smiled.

1961 MURDER REMAINS UNSOLVED

Kingston—January 1995

The daughter of a slain prison guard—knifed to death thirty-four years ago—wept in court as a judge stayed a murder charge against a prime suspect in the case.

"I think the justice just failed us this afternoon," Daphne Jenkins said after Judge Thomas Lally ruled in favor of a defense argument that bringing Ralph Cochrane to trial after a thirty-four-year delay was unconstitutional.

Cochrane, sixty-eight, was charged in 1993 in the stabbing death of Kingston Penitentiary guard William Wentworth. Wentworth was killed in a prison washroom in November 1961 while dozens of inmates slept nearby. The guard suffered eleven knife wounds.

No one cooperated with investigators in the case and although Cochrane had been charged in 1962, the Crown didn't proceed with the prosecution. Evidence against Cochrane came mainly from Edwin Alonzo Boyd, eighty-one, one of the country's most notorious bank robbers.

Judge Lally said there had been an "unreasonable delay" in bringing Cochrane before the courts. Cochrane is still in prison, serving life for a wave of bank robberies. He will be eligible for release in 1997.

Daphne Jenkins, one of the victim's two grown children, said she'd hoped to put her father's death to rest: "We as a family need the answers and now we're not going to get them."

Although a stay effectively means the charge has been tossed out, the Crown has one year to refile.

JOHN JAMES ROONEY

Charlottetown—January 1995

In January 1995, after one of the longest and most expensive trials in Prince Edward Island history, John James Rooney was found not criminally responsible for the stabbing murder of a Charlottetown man.

But Rooney, 34, would have rather gone to jail as a killer than to a psychiatric hospital as a madman: "Psychiatrists shouldn't have been brought into this case at all," he told the PEI Supreme Court, saying society is trying to prevent him from being himself. "Do I fit in? Do I even want to fit in in a ward at a hospital? That's not the place for a sane mind!"

During Rooney's trial court was told he attacked and killed James Acorn in September 1993. Acorn was stabbed seven times with a butcher knife and a hatchet. Rooney, who had a previous criminal record and was on probation at the time of the slaying, elected to defend himself because his legal aid lawyers had abandoned him and said he was crazy.

Testimony showed Rooney had been diagnosed as suffering from either schizophrenia or a delusional disorder.

But the bearded, pony-tailed defendant conducted his own defense, often jacking up the level of tension in the courtroom. On one occasion he picked up the hatchet from the evidence table went nose-to-nose with a terrified witness. Justice David Jenkins warned him to ask questions from his chair and to keep his hands off the exhibits.

When Rooney refused to take notes on a day's proceedings, the court was tied up the next day when the tapes of the testimony had to be played for him.

The trial, expected to take a week when it began on August 29, 1994, ran to twelve weeks and racked up heavy expenses. Among them: a legal aid lawyer to assist in Rooney in his defense and extra salary and service costs for the Crown attorney. Because Rooney was considered dangerous, two police officers were in court every day. When Justice Jenkins felt the air quality of the courtroom was not suitable for such a long hearing, he had the trial moved for two months to a hearing room in a nearby building. Cost of the move: $125 per day.

In December 1994 Rooney—originally charged with second-degree murder—was found guilty of manslaughter. A month later Justice Jenkins found the convicted man wasn't criminally responsible for the killing because he suffered from a mental disorder. The finding means Rooney would not be convicted of manslaughter, nor would he have a criminal record. Because PEI doesn't have a mental hospital with high enough security to house the criminally insane, Rooney was expected to be sent to an out of province facility.

Jenkins said Rooney represents a high risk because of his previous violent acts, his alcohol abuse, his denial of mental illness and guilt in the Acorn murder, and his assertions that he had killed other victims.

It wasn't the first time Rooney had been found mentally unstable. In 1991, he had been involuntarily committed to hospital after he was found unfit to stand trial after a rooming-house tenant was attacked with a hatchet.

And in March 1995, Rooney—housed at the Nova Scotia Hospital's forensic unit—was charged after another patient was attacked.

A RITUAL DEATH

Cambridge—January 1995

Police arrested the mother, grandmother and neighbors of a two-year-old girl who died, apparently during an exorcism.

Waterloo Regional Police said Kira Canhoto was found dead in her Cambridge home in mid-January. Coroner Hank Nykamp said she died when the flow of blood to her brain was "restricted ...probably just by a restraining arm around the head, holding the child." He added: "It probably wouldn't take long for the brain to swell."

"We've determined this was the result of an attempt to rid her of a demon," police said.

As neighbors stood near the Canhoto family home remembering Kira, a child with a sweet smile and big brown eyes, they shook their heads in disbelief. "I just don't understand why," one woman said sadly.

Kira's grandmother, Ana Maria Canhoto, 43, one of those charged with manslaughter in the death, was a member of Our Lady of Lourdes church before becoming part of a prayer group. The group speaks in tongues, and members believe they have special powers.

In mid-June, Ana Maria Canhoto pleaded guilty to manslaughter. Crown Attorney Peter Speyer tolod the court that the child had been forced to drink water to rid her of the devil. "The devil fought back and the baby kicked and held her teeth together," he said, adding Canhoto squeezed Kira's cheeks, forcing her mouth open and repeatedly pouring cups of water into the girl. Canhoto thought the exorcism was working when Kira began vomiting, expelling the devil. The convicted woman was remanded for sentencing.

FARMER'S FIELD DUMPING GROUND FOR SERIAL KILLER

Saskatoon—January 1995

The autumn of 1994 must have seemed like the season of death to residents in the Saskatoon area when police found the dumping grounds of a serial killer.

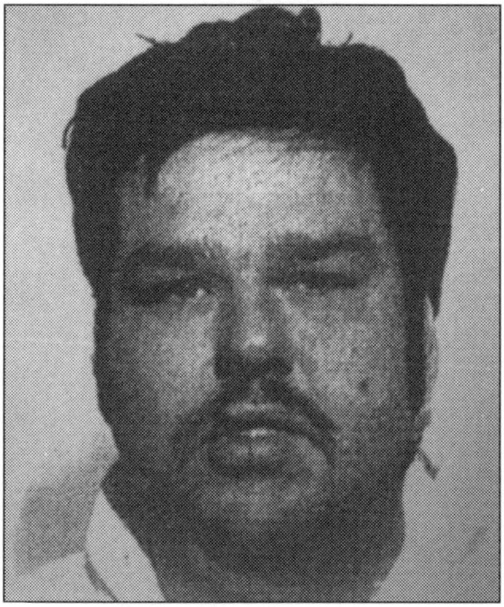

John Martin Crawford

As in most major cases involving repeat murderers, the investigation was sparked by an unhappy accident. In early October a hunter stumbled across a set of skeletal remains in a farmer's field south of the Moon Lake Golf Course, sixteen kilometers south of Saskatoon.

The bones were those of a young woman. The remains had been at the scene for perhaps two years.

An RCMP examination of the area turned up two more sets of remains about three weeks later. These were approximately thirty meters from the first discovery: a finding that pointed to the tradecraft of a serial killer, probably someone familiar with the area; someone who used the location as a private graveyard.

Remains two and three were also of young women. Forensic examination and detailed work by anthropologist Ernie Walker showed the victims were native Canadian women, all in their early twenties.

(In the first month of the case, police were dealt a wild card: a fourth woman, Janet Sylvestre, thirty-seven, was found asphyxiated west of Saskatoon. She had been dead only a day, and a plastic bag had been secured over her head. Ultimately, detectives found no link between Sylvestre and the three bush victims. RCMP said their investigation into Sylvestre's death was continuing.)

Led by RCMP Sergeant Colin Crocker, a task force of investigators began to work on the two-year-old cases. They went to a list of almost five hundred missing people to look for subjects who matched the victims in age, race and body size.

Working from Walker's profiles, police artists produced sketches to show what the women looked like before they were slain.

By mid-January, working from the profiles and dental records, police had identities on their victims: Calinda Waterhen, twenty-two; Eva Taysup, thirty; and Shelley Napope, sixteen. All were connected to the 20th Street bar scene.

Serial killing investigations are traditionally long affairs, which often take years to reach the point of arrest, but on January 20, 1995, in a copyrighted story, reporters Warren Goulding and Terry Craig of the *Star-Phoenix* revealed that the murder task force had arrested a suspect.

A team of eight officers armed with a search warrant picked up John Martin Crawford, thirty-two, at his mother's group home at Avenue L and 21st Street on the west side of the city.

The group home, a residence for indigent men, was searched and some evidence was removed. Investigators concentrated on Crawford's room, and they checked the deep freezer.

Crawford's mother told the reporters, "[I] can't believe it, he's a good boy."

A man who lived in the same house as Crawford said he was a quiet man who slept during the day and got up and went out for coffee at night. He said he sometimes went down to 20th Street.

Crawford was charged with three counts of first-degree murder. He was remanded in custody.

Asked if the suspect was connected to the Janet Sylvestre slaying, prosecutor Terry Hinz refused to comment, but said the probe into her murder was continuing.

CONVICTION IN GIANT MINE BLAST

Yellowknife—January 1995

On January 20, 1995, Roger Warren was convicted of nine counts of second-degree murder in the 1992 Giant mine blast in Yellowknife.

The explosion occurred in the midst of a bitter strike that began seven months earlier when Royal Oak Mines locked out union staff and brought in replacement workers.

On September 18, 1992, a massive detonation 230 meters below ground instantly killed three replacement workers and six union members who had crossed the picket line.

A lengthy investigation into the mass murder ended when Warren confessed to police. He later tried to recant his confession, saying he only confessed because he was depressed. He was initially charged with first-degree murder and was instead convicted on nine counts of second-degree murder.

His defense counsel has appealed both the conviction and the sentence of life in prison with no parole for twenty years. The appeal is based on Justice Mark de Weert's decision to allow into evidence Warren's confession that he set the bomb.

The Crown, too, is appealing the case. They believe Justice de Weert gave improper definitions of first- and second-degree murder and manslaughter to the jury.

In mid-May 1995, three Yellowknife union activists used their newsletter to raise financial support for Warren. The two-page newsletter claims he was falsely convicted in the case: "This was a sick, gross and unjust verdict. Roger is innocent. Please help."

THE PISTOL-PACKING SOCIALITE

Calgary—January 1995

In early January 1995 Dorothy Joudrie was named "hostess with the mostest" after throwing a soirée for one hundred of Calgary's most prominent socialites.

Two weeks later, on January 21, her estranged husband was treated for multiple gunshot wounds at Dorothy's posh condo and the hostess with the mostest was led away in handcuffs to face an attempted murder charge.

Earl Joudrie, sixty, was admitted to hospital where he ordered a news blackout on information about his condition. He had bullets in his back and he was expected to survive.

The *Financial Post*'s "1995 Directory of Directors," a who's who of big business circles, listed Joudrie as chairman of the board of Canadian Tire, Gulf Canada Resources and Algoma Steel. He sits on the board of several major Canadian corporations.

Paramedics were called to a reported shooting at Dorothy Joudrie's luxury condominium home at the exclusive Bearspaw Country Club just before 11 a.m. on a quiet Saturday morning. Earl Joudrie was found collapsed on the garage floor of the building. He was treated where he fell as heavily armed RCMP and Calgary police moved in to secure the building. Moments later they arrested Dorothy Joudrie, the victim's estranged wife.

Joudrie was flown by air ambulance to Foothills Hospital in Calgary where he underwent surgery.

Police revealed little about the incident, but said it "was not an accidental shooting." A firearm was recovered.

The shooting rocked Canada's upper-crust business community but no one had any motive for the violence.

GANG OF HIGH-TECH ROVING BANDITS ARRESTED

London—January 1995

A probe into a string of armed robberies in southwestern Ontario exploded into an investigation into a wave of handgun violence that left two men dead.

Three London area men were arrested after a joint task force made up of local, provincial and federal police officers conducted an undercover probe into several violent holdups in the southwestern part of the province.

The roving bandits used disguises, stolen cars, phony drivers' licenses and radio equipment to monitor police activity. They carried high-powered weapons and wore body armor during several of the robberies. During one stickup a store customer was shot in both legs.

As the gang's crime wave continued, police in Durham Region east of Toronto began investigating the back-to-back homicides of a pair of men, one of them the owner of a gun shop.

Police said Roger Pardy, forty-three, was fatally shot in the head when his shop was raided by a gang on September 14, 1994. Three other men in the store were wounded by gunfire.

Within hours of the robbery police received a missing persons report for Kenneth Thomas, fifty-five, of Pickering, Ontario. Police later discovered that his burgundy Chevrolet Caprice had been used in the robbery–homicide. Thomas, apparently an innocent victim of a carjacking, was found dead on January 21, 1995. He had been shot.

After the three London men were arrested, police revealed they were investigating ties between the Durham Region crimes and the southwestern Ontario robberies. Two .45-caliber handguns used by the gang were traced to the gunshop robbery–homicide, detectives said.

DNA CLEARS MORIN IN JESSOP SEX SLAYING

Queensville—January 1995

On January 23, 1995, the Ontario Court of Appeal acquitted Guy Paul Morin in the sex slaying of nine-year-old Christine Jessop, ending one of Canada's longest-running and most controversial murder cases.

Jessop disappeared from Queensville, Ontario, north of Toronto, on October 3, 1984. Her body was found in a farmer's field on New Year's Eve. She had been sexually assaulted and stabbed to death.

Homicide detectives quickly centered their probe on Jessop's neighbor, Guy Paul Morin. In the spring of 1985, Morin was arrested and charged with murder. He was held in custody until he went to trial in 1986. A jury acquitted him, but the Crown appealed the acquittal and Morin underwent a second trial, which lasted nine months. He was convicted on July 30, 1992.

He appealed the conviction and, on the eve of his appeal in January 1995, a DNA test, comparing semen found at the murder scene with Morin's blood, found they didn't match.

Morin was instantly set free. But his ten-year saga at the hands of the judicial system came under scrutiny. Attorney-General Marion Boyd said she wanted a full public inquiry into the issues raised in the case. The murder probe was turned over to a team of crack detectives from the Metropolitan Toronto Police homicide squad for reinvestigation.

The Jessop murder team was quickly set up, but after waiting three months for government action on the inquiry, Morin's lawyers were angry that a commission hadn't been formed. They said that among the areas needing examination are: the conduct of the provincially funded Centre of Forensic Sciences, which lost evidence; the failure by police and prosecutors to disclose evidence that might have worked on Morin's behalf; and the reliance on jailhouse informants.

SCHOOLS FIGHT BACK

Scarborough—January 1995

The school board in the Metro Toronto city of Scarborough struck back against violence in the classroom with a zero-tolerance policy.

In January 1995 the tenth student, in the school's first year of strict enforcement, was booted for pulling a pair of scissors during a fight at the Bendale Business and Technical Institute. The eighteen-year-old male's behavior so disrupted the school that "his presence would be injurious" to other students, the school board found.

Walter Freel, a member of the city of Etobicoke's school board, said violence in schools is "very scary," adding violence was becoming an acceptable form of aggression.

Education officials and police noted a rise in reports of violence at many Metropolitan Toronto schools. In one case a sixteen-year-old was turfed out for life after firing a paper clip with a rubber band into the eye of another student. The sixteen-year-old was already facing several charges, including aggravated assault and making death threats.

And it isn't just high schools where violence is growing. A school official said more and more children aged seven to ten are getting into fights and refusing to stop when teachers intervene.

YOUTH STATS

According to Metropolitan Toronto police statistics, the number of young offenders aged twelve to seventeen arrested for assault-related crimes steadily increased between 1990 and 1994.

1990

Assault 977

Assault causing bodily harm (ABH) and assault with weapon 494

1991

Assault 1,053

ABH and assault with weapon 484

1992

Assault 1,096

ABH and assault with weapon 524

1993

Assault 1,306

ABH and assault with weapon 639

1994

Assault 1,417

ABH and assault with weapon 630

MONTREAL ACTOR MURDERED

THE MURDER OF popular Montreal actor Richard Niquette led to accusations that the federal government was failing to protect those who were victims of crime because of their sexual orientation.

Niquette, forty-four, died moments after being stabbed at about four o'clock on the morning of February 19. He sustained a knife wound to the heart. His killers stole about $300 before leaving the mortally wounded actor dying in a basement apartment on Cuvillier Street. The victim managed to get outside to the street where he collapsed, naked and covered in blood.

Niquette had had supporting roles in several movies and was also a stage actor. He was best known for his role as a sports reporter on *Lance et Compte*, a Radio-Canada TV program.

Two men were charged in connection with the murder. A detective said he believed the motive for the slaying was a combination of gay hatred and robbery.

Niquette was the nineteenth member of Montreal's gay community to be killed within a four-year period, and the city's Committee for Lesbians and Gays Against Violence lashed out at the federal government for not bringing in a promised Criminal Code amendment to protect victims of crimes targeted for their sexual orientation.

"Niquette's blood is on their hands," Douglas Buckley-Couvrette charged, adding: "I'm not saying Niquette wouldn't have been killed if the amendment had been made, but it might have served as a deterrent. It's time the government sent out a message to society that crimes against homosexuals will no longer be tolerated."

He said attacks on gay people are hate crimes and demanded that the government act quickly. "Are they waiting for a twentieth body?" he asked.

In June 1994 another nasty gay-related murder case ended in a murder conviction for a thirty-one-year-old man.

The victim in the case, Warren Eling, was the rector of Montreal's St. James the Apostle Anglican Church. The fifty-four-year-old former Toronto pastor habituated both cities' gay communities and often cruised the bars.

On November 1, 1993, Eling picked up a young man named Danny McIlwaine who was hustling in the downtown gay village. Eling took McIlwaine home and paid him to engage in sex. When McIlwaine left, Eling gave him his phone number and invited him to call.

A week later the men spoke on the phone and Eling drove over and picked up McIlwaine. Within hours the priest was dead.

Police found him sprawled on his back in the rectory. He was naked and bound to his brass bed with his underwear, his arms outstretched as in a crucifixion. A facecloth was spread over his genitals, and a yellow belt from his bathrobe was wrapped five times around his neck and tightly knotted to the bed head.

Gone from the rectory was Eling's computer, his CD player and a VCR. McIlwaine pawned the goods and fled to Toronto in Eling's car. He dumped the vehicle, but left a pop can inside with his fingerprint on it. Police matched the print against their files and came up with McIlwaine's name. He'd returned to Montreal and was arrested in St. Luc Hospital, where he'd been taken after trying to commit suicide by drinking antifreeze.

He told police the death was the result of autoerotic asphyxiation, a sadomasochist ritual known as "scarfing." He said Eling was into bondage and wanted to try something new.

McIlwaine's lawyer offered the autoerotic defense but on June 1, 1994, a jury found McIlwaine guilty of first-degree murder.

In a finely crafted news feature, *Montreal Gazette* reporter Alan Hustak quoted a Toronto clergyman who knew the victim well: "Warren's failings were human, yet he was not entirely blameless for what happened to him. He was not an innocent victim. Like the boy who killed him, he 'followed too much the devices and desires of his own heart,' and has 'done those things which he ought not to have done.'"

THE LARGEST KIDDIE PORN PROBE

London—February 1995

A collection of child pornography found dumped into the Sauble River near London, Ontario, in 1993 led to what became the largest kiddie porn probe in Canadian history.

In August 1993, changes to the law made the simple possession of child pornography a crime. Police believe the new law led a collector to dispose of his personal collection. When a youth came across the tapes, he took home forty cassettes from the river. His mother viewed them and was shocked to find images of men and boys committing homosexual acts. She contacted police and, after searching the river, officers wound up with another fifty-three tapes.

When the police examined the tapes they recognized some of the youths involved and at least one of the adult males.

Within two months London city police had found and charged two men. Thomas Jewell, forty-two, and Gary Gramlick, fifty-nine, faced several charges ranging from possession and manufacture of child pornography to sex offenses. Both were convicted; Jewell got fifteen years and Gramlick got ten years.

At a news conference police exhibited almost two hundred cassettes and some video-production equipment. Police Chief Julian Fantino told reporters there was "a very substantial ring" of suspects in the investigation "whose sole purpose is to corrupt children."

A task force—Operation Scoop—was set up and for the next six months detectives interviewed dozens of young males, aged between eight and seventeen. Operation Scoop arrested thirty men, including a university librarian, a transit driver, a politician and a former school principal.

In May 1994 after a teen gave police information about a high school teacher, investigators raided the man's home. They seized more than eight hundred videos and hundreds of magazines and photographs.

London police went to the Ontario government for help in

continuing the investigation. With aid from the solicitor-general's department, another task force was set up in July. It included members of the Ontario Provincial Police Project P antipornography unit. The task force was dubbed Project Guardian.

The Guardian squad interviewed more than seventy-five boys and youths, ranging in age from eight to seventeen. By early 1995 police had picked up fifty-seven men on four hundred and fifty charges relating to the porn ring.

The investigation then evolved into a battle between police and gay rights activists, who pointed out that not all the tapes seized from the high school teacher were pornographic. The teacher has filed suit against police.

Gay activists also say there were no eight-year-old boys involved in the Guardian project; police say there were four children of that age, but they say the boys were too young to testify in the court cases without being damaged. The youngest child to testify was eleven years old.

By the beginning of the summer of 1995 police and some members of the gay community were still at loggerheads over the Project Guardian investigation. Gay activists are accusing Fantino and the police force of homophobia and they're arguing that the news media were either sucked in by police or were coopted. Police maintain their investigation was correctly run. They say they were conducting a criminal probe, not a witch hunt.

Project Guardian's one-year mandate ended in July 1995.

A STABBING FRENZY

Winnipeg—February 1995

It was the most public of murders: on May 6, 1994, in broad daylight, Bruce Stewner chased his estranged wife, Kelly-Lynn, along Portage Avenue in Winnipeg, repeatedly stabbing her with a knife. Stewner, plunging the knife into his wife's back asked: "How do you like that, Kelly?"

Several witnesses, among them an off-duty policeman, watched in horror as Stewner, on top of Kelly-Lynn, continued stabbing her.

When one man approached the couple, Stewner stopped his stabbing frenzy and asked: "Do you want some, too?" Then he continued the fatal attack on his wife before running away.

The off-duty cop chased him and found him nearby still clutching his weapon and surrounded by men armed with boards. Stewner yelled, "I'll take you all on and kill you like I killed her." He was overpowered and taken into custody.

After two turbulent years of marriage and a frantic effort to evade her stalking husband, Kelly-Lynn, 23, was dead of more than twenty knife wounds.

Stewner went to trial in February 1995. His lawyer said the accused man was provoked to murder when Kelly-Lynn told him she had had a love affair with his older brother.

After hearing five days of testimony, it took the jury two hours to find him guilty of second-degree murder.

In an interview with *Winnipeg Sun* crime reporter Mike D'Amour, Stewner said he'd been in a jealous rage when he killed Kelly-Lynn, and that they'd made a suicide pact. They were on their way to kill themselves when Kelly-Lynn began taunting him about having had a lengthy affair with his brother. Describing himself as "your average kinda guy," Stewner insisted he loved his wife, but he "just lost it."

"I lost all sense of control....Everything just went black. Voices sounded very far away. It was like somebody else was doing it. I was on the outside looking in," he told D'Amour.

CONVICT'S VICTIM GETS $394,000

Gravenhurst—February 1995

A woman who was raped, beaten, choked and left for dead by an escaped convict was awarded a record payment by an Ontario court.

The forty-eight-year-old housewife from the Muskoka area, north of Metro Toronto, was attacked after Philippe Clement, thirty-five, a convicted sex killer serving a life sentence, walked away from a fenceless prison facility in September 1992.

Clement made his way to the victim's home where he attacked her. Court was told the woman's blood was spattered on the walls and floors of the home. She had been beaten so badly, her husband testified, she was "almost unrecognizable."

"She was covered in blood, with a gaping gash to the bone," he said. "Her whole head and neck were swollen to grotesque proportions."

He said there were bloody handprints on the walls and blood on the telephone. "In the biggest single area there was so much blood it soaked through the carpet and congealed to three-eighths of an inch in height. The bloodstains were unbelievable."

He said his wife kept repeating: "I'm alive, I'm alive."

Clement was captured a short time later near the home of one of his female prison guards, a woman he'd become obsessed with. He pleaded guilty to aggravated sexual assault and attempted murder. He received two life sentences.

But the victim's family was outraged that a prisoner with Clement's history had been transferred to the minimum security Beaver Creek facility. They sued Clement and Correctional Service of Canada for more than $3 million in damages, claiming Clement was too dangerous for the lightly guarded facility.

His past record showed he received a life sentence for stabbing a female law student to death in Montreal in 1977. The victim, a stranger to Clement, was stabbed eighty times.

He had assaulted about twenty women since he was twelve years old. His fifteen-year-old girlfriend escaped death because "while I was strangling her, with her lips she was saying, I love you, Clement said."

In February 1995 the Gravenhurst woman was awarded $394,000 by Madam Justice Susan Lang, who found fault with Corrections Canada. It was the first time the prison system was found liable for not taking appropriate care to prevent escapes and failing to notify the public.

The victim and her family left Ontario and are living in British Columbia.

LAWYER ON THE RUN

Toronto—February 1995

The day before his forty-eighth birthday, lawyer John Jaffey was told he would spend the next five blowing out candles in the penitentiary.

Jaffey pleaded guilty February 27, 1995, to nine charges, including fraud, theft, money laundering and using a forged passport.

The previous July had started well. Jaffey was a new millionaire, with $2.3 million and a ticket for Australia. Two weeks later he was surrendering quietly to Australian policemen who surrounded him at a Sydney bank.

Jaffey had been reported missing by his wife after he failed to return from a trip to Ottawa. Jaffey lived in Toronto with his wife and their three children. The lawyer handled real estate and some family law. He was a pretty low-key man, constantly working. It wasn't like him to just disappear.

An investigation quickly determined the lost lawyer had taken off with a large amount of his clients' funds, including $162,000 belonging to his elderly mother, Irene. The Canadian Cancer Society, the Heart and Stroke Foundation and the Canadian Hearing Society all lost money to Jaffey. A single mom lost her life savings of $7,212. There were at least two dozen victims, most of them scammed when Jaffey registered discharged mortgages with forged documents.

Metro police kicked off an international manhunt and, acting on a tip, notified detectives in Sydney, Australia, that Jaffey was on their turf. The lawyer was taken down at a bank as he deposited $129,000. He surrendered quietly.

In his hotel room police found travelers' cheques worth $120,000 in British, Mexican, Italian and Australian currency. The passport of a dead man, Morley Shelman of Toronto, was also seized.

The well-traveled lawyer didn't fight extradition and was returned to Toronto.

The judge at his trial was told the scheme had been ten years in the planning. Jaffey offered remorse: “I feel intense sorrow for all my victims and all the hardships I’ve caused,” the tearful lawyer said. “I’ve had a guilty conscience for several years.”

Justice Hugh Locke dismissed Jaffey’s statement, noting if he was truly remorseful, he’d have taken the subway to a police station instead of a plane to Australia.

Crown attorney Jim Atkinson asked for a five-year term: “It doesn’t get much lower than this.”

THE VAMPIRE STRIKES AGAIN

DONALD "VINCE" KUNTZ, convicted of cutting a woman and drinking her blood in 1992, tried to use the "too much to drink" defense in 1995 after he was charged with chewing on another woman's face.

Kuntz, twenty-seven, was sentenced to four years in prison after he was convicted of aggravated assault on Marjorie Robeiro, also twenty-seven. Mr. Justice Hugh Locke described Kuntz, a one-time singer for the rock band Infernal Majesty, as "a mad dog" whose "whole life bespeaks violence."

The court was told Kuntz and some friends had met Robeiro at the Death in the Underground bar in Toronto in September 1994. The group went to the Sanctuary-Vampire Sex Bar where Kuntz pulled his girlfriend's hair and made her scream. Robeiro, also sitting at the table, poured a beer over Kuntz's head and he attacked her. He put his mouth over her eye and bit down, tearing through the skin.

Kuntz, a minister's son, was wearing a dog collar. He was arrested. At the police station he ripped out a ceiling fan and some tiles and tried to escape, wearing only his underwear. Before he could get away he became involved in a struggle with Constable Dale Gibbons. During the battle Kuntz tried to chew on Gibbons's ear "like a dog trying to bite at a piece of meat," the court was told. Police overpowered Kuntz.

He was on bail and probation at the time of the attack and had eight violence-related offenses among his two dozen convictions.

Among his previous convictions was the attack on Halloween 1992 on Sally Fahy, twenty-two. Kuntz offered to buy Fahy a drink if she'd let him suck her blood. She agreed, and later that night as they were kissing in her bedroom, Kuntz held her hand to the wall and sliced her wrist. "He grabbed my wrist and held it to his mouth and made drinking noises," Fahy reported.

As a friend took Fahy to hospital, Kuntz was licking spilled blood off the bedroom floor.

Kuntz was arrested the next day. While he was in custody Fahy wrote him love letters and accepted several collect calls from Kuntz while he was in jail.

He was convicted and sent to jail for a day. The judge cited Fahy's conduct in the case.

During the Robeiro trial Fahy, now Kuntz's girlfriend, showed up in court and said she hoped he'd be acquitted.

The accused's lawyer, Tony Bryant, tried to persuade the court that Kuntz, who had drunk twenty-one ounces of whiskey and sixty ounces of beer, was too drunk to know what he was doing.

Justice Locke rejected the claim and sent Kuntz to jail for four years. He was also convicted of assaulting police, escaping custody and public mischief.

CASSANDRA

Toronto—March 1995

During their eighteen-month relationship, Ian James Bell beat Cassandra Hawke to within an inch of her life. On the evening of November 29, 1993, he beat her the other inch. In the middle of March 1995, with his second-degree murder charge bargained down to manslaughter, he was sentenced to seven years and three months in prison. After fourteen months he'd be eligible for day parole.

Cassandra Hawke, twenty-six, was beaten to death with a metal baseball bat, golf clubs and bamboo sticks. According to the *Toronto Sun*'s Michele Mandel, who viewed the autopsy photographs, Hawke's entire body was battered. Pathologist Dr. John Deck, who had seen twenty-seven years worth of autopsies, told Mandel: "It's the worse beating I've ever seen, and I've seen lots of them."

Previous assaults had left lesions on Hawke's heart, and it was that weakness that led to her death during the 1993 attack.

Hawke and Bell met in 1992 after she'd come out of a long-term relationship. She fell in love with Bell, in spite of warnings about him.

His first wife, Jacqueline, was beaten for nine years before she left him. On one occasion he kicked her in the head with steel-toed construction boots. Every time he was charged he talked her into lying for him. He was diagnosed as a manic-depressive but refused to get treatment.

But Hawke was in love. The couple got engaged and she became pregnant. One day she showed up at work, covered in bruises. She told a friend she'd been in a car accident, but then admitted she'd been beaten. She ignored her friend's urgings to get help and to get out of the relationship.

When she was eight months' pregnant she was thrown down the stairs. The couple's home became the scene of numerous reports of fighting and disturbances, and Hawke cut herself off from her friends and family.

On November 29, 1993, the neighbors heard yet another fight, heard Bell ordering Hawke to clean herself off.

At 6:32 p.m., Bell called 911. Emergency crews found him in the kitchen, crying over Hawke's naked, bleeding body. An autopsy showed she died of heart failure.

Although charged with second-degree murder, Bell agreed to plead guilty to manslaughter.

PIZZA LINEUP

Montreal—March 1995

Montreal police who tried to take a slice out of crime wound up on the receiving end of a complaint after they conned several youths into participating in a lineup.

Police Commander Jacques Roger admitted some of the nine black youths may not have been aware that they were being used in a lineup after officers went to a high school and offered the students pizza and pop.

At the police station the teens were put into a room where they were part of a lineup during a criminal investigation.

The school's principal said he had refused police permission to use his students as extras in the lineup. A short time later at least six police cruisers arrived at the school, and police offered the snack.

When the teens got to the police station, they were told the food wasn't ready. They were put into a room with three suspects and viewed through a two-way mirror.

Outraged school officials demanded a probe. They quickly got an apology and change of policy from the police chief.

MISSING; THEN FOUND

Ottawa—March 1995

It had all the earmarks of a murder mystery: a missing woman, gone for seven months; a massive police search and criminal investigation; a $10,000 reward.

But when it ended, Diana Vallee turned up alive and said she had disappeared because of a domestic dispute.

Vallee, thirty-seven, vanished August 12, 1994, after working late at her office on Murray Street, in Ottawa. She had spoken to her husband, Andre, and said she'd be late, probably eight o'clock. She said she planned to take a taxi home. She called Blue Line Cab at seven-thirty but never got in a cab.

When she failed to show up by the following day, Andre reported his wife of nine years missing.

Initially police considered Andre a suspect in the case, but he passed a lie-detector test with flying colors. He said he wasn't an abusive husband, but admitted he had struck his wife once during the generally stable marriage.

Detectives were assigned to the case and a trace on Vallee's credit and bank cards showed no usage. Two appeals were made through the Crime Stoppers organization, but neither turned up any clues. In December Vallee's family offered a $10,000 reward for information, but again nothing turned up.

Seven months after she vanished, Vallee spoke with Ottawa detectives by phone and said she was unharmed. She said she didn't wish to be located or have her location known by anyone, police said. "She left on her own volition. As far as police know, she acted on her own and informed no one of her plans," Staff-Sergeant Rick Murphy said.

In an interview with the CBC, Vallee said she left out of fear of her domineering husband and the control she said he had over her. "I finally realized how he was controlling me," she told the CBC. "And he was controlling me. Most of my paycheck was going to him. I was paying rent on his duplex. Everything was his."

Andre Vallee said he was not going to drop his wife, adding he wanted her to get help.

RADARCOP

Scarborough—March 1995

An Ontario Provincial Police officer who parked his photo radar van in a fire zone got more and less than he bargained for.

Constable Perry Bernard of the Downsview OPP detachment said he parked his van in the fire zone of a Scarborough apartment building on March 18, 1995, while he delivered a summons. When he returned, he found his van had been towed. He got the van from the pound but wasn't forced to pay the two hundred dollars in fines, towing and storage charges.

Bylaw enforcement officer Richard Penney said he enforced the parking rules to the letter of the law because of his dislike for photo radar.

An internal investigation found Bernard had not stopped to deliver a summons—he was on his lunch break. He was docked twenty hours' pay—about $500— as a corrective measure by the Professional Standards Branch.

RACIAL STRIFE HEATS UP THE NATION'S CAPITAL

Ottawa—March 1995

What should have been a routine attempt to arrest a man at a downtown Ottawa housing complex led to racial tension, lawsuits and the death of a policeman.

On March 20, 1995, Constable Shawn Wilson was among a

group of officers who responded to a call from a woman who said someone was trying to beat down her door. When police arrived, the woman's former boyfriend, thirty-four-year-old Wayne Johnson, ran from the scene. He was pursued, then caught, by the officers but managed to break free. He either jumped or fell into the nearby Rideau River. Johnson went under the icy surface, swollen with spring run-off. Moments later, he bobbed to the surface and began to float down river. Ripping car seats from their cruisers, the officers threw two into the river for Johnson to use as flotation devices. But Johnson disappeared into the water. A search failed to turn up his body. Five days later, it was found just meters from where Johnson disappeared.

Johnson's family and members of the city's Jamaican community criticized police handling of the case, and at Johnson's funeral a speaker warned that black people lived in "a hostile situation." Ottawa had recently been racked by other incidents involving police and the black community.

The provincial Special Investigations Unit is called in on all cases involving police-related injury or death to the public. They found that Johnson had been pepper-sprayed during the pursuit. The SIU did not release a report on the case, but their investigation indicated that Constable Wilson "had nothing to worry about," Ottawa Chief Brian Ford said.

But on May 10 Wilson, who was on stress leave after Johnson's death and unaware he'd been exonerated, put a shotgun to his head and committed suicide.

Five hundred angry, bitter police officers attended his funeral. Senior officers and members of the press were kept out of the church where the services were held. Police brass and the SIU were castigated for their handling of the investigation.

HACKER CHARGED

Toronto—March 1995

A suspected hacker faces numerous charges of computer fraud and computer-related mischief after the RCMP probed one of the biggest cases of hacking in Canada.

Adam Shiffman, twenty, of Metro Toronto, was arrested in late

March after several computers were hacked into. Among those victimized were the Ontario Institute for Studies in Education and several university and community college computer systems, including those of the University of Toronto and the University of Western Ontario.

Police believe the man then worked his way through several U.S. universities, including Harvard and Princeton, and snooped around government files.

The extent of the damage hasn't been determined.

"DEPRAVED CRIMINAL ACTS"

Toronto—March 1995

A Metro Toronto area man who "stole the innocence" of his common law wife's children was sent to prison for four years.

For his "repetitious, depraved, criminal acts" Joseph Young, fifty-two, was slammed by Mr. Justice Victor Paisley in the Ontario Court on March 30. "I don't think there could be a more severe effect on them psychologically if there had been full sexual intercourse," Justice Paisley told the twice-divorced drunk.

The court was told that Young was living with his common law wife and her twelve-year-old daughter and eleven-year-old son in Newmarket, north of Toronto, in 1982 when the children were forced to perform oral sex on him.

"It seems every time we were alone something would happen," the daughter told the court. "It seemed to happen when my mom wasn't around," her brother said.

In referring to one incident, in which the boy watched his sister being abused by Young, Justice Paisley described the scene as one of "stark horror."

Young's lawyer, who said his client has high blood pressure and a pacemaker, said he would appeal the prison sentence.

NAME-CALLING TEEN FATALLY STABBED

Port Coquitlam—March 1995

The fatal stabbing of a teenager—reportedly for calling someone a "geek"—at a Port Coquitlam lacrosse field sparked the mayor into vowing action against youth violence.

Jody Alfred Larsen, nineteen, was stabbed to death in a public lacrosse box at May Hill Road and Wilson Avenue in Port Coquitlam, British Columbia, on March 31, 1995. He had been knifed at least a dozen times.

Police believe Larsen and four friends got into a name-calling confrontation with another group of youths. There had been talk of a rumble at the park before the attack. In all, as many as sixty youths were involved in the incident.

When the dust settled, Larsen was dying in a pool of blood.

A seventeen-year-old youth was arrested and charged with murder.

Larsen and the accused didn't know each other, RCMP Corporal Gil Campbell said. "It was stupid," Campbell added. "The mentality is if kids just look at someone in the wrong way it can end up in a stabbing." He said the rumble was sparked when Larsen called another youth a geek, and the second youth vowed to come back with his friends.

Mayor Len Traboulay said he planned to get tough on teens who idle around local streets. Traboulay arranged a meeting with police and youths to prevent congregating by teens at convenience stores and gas stations.

"The youngster who died was stabbed fifteen times," he said. "That is a heinous crime. We in Port Coquitlam are not given to that kind of violence."

The Larsen slaying was the third murder involving "group dynamics" in the city since 1992. One youth was stabbed dead that year, and in August 1994 a thirty-one-year-old man was beaten to death outside a city convenience store after an altercation with a group of teens.

RUBBER BREASTS

Toronto—March 1995

A Toronto cross dresser turned himself into a woman. And later turned himself in to the police.

On March 28 Metro officers reported the bizarre case of a

man who wore a wig, makeup, halter top and rubber breasts in the changing room of the Etobicoke Olympium swimming pool.

The man would arrive at the pool as a man, then change into a woman in the basement. Then he'd make his way to the women's changing room, where he ogled young women as they arrived at and left the pool.

In December 1994 three fourteen-year-olds became uncomfortable under the man's gawking. When they took a closer look at the big-boned, masculine "woman," they realized she was a man and began screaming. The intruder ran from the area.

During the next four months police received numerous complaints from women, and at the end of March they charged a twenty-six-year-old suspect after he surrendered.

Police seized a tote bag containing a pair of rubber breasts, a bra, black spandex pants, a halter top, makeup and a brown wig. The accused is charged with mischief and wearing a disguise.

ViVi Leimonis

VIVI LEIMONIS UPDATE

NO ONE MURDER is more serious than another: the death of a single citizen is a piece ripped from the fabric that makes up society. In spite of police reaction, public outcry or media outrage, no life can be given value beyond another.

Yet some murders strike a chord deep in the heart of a city, and the slaying of Georgina "ViVi" Leimonis rang loud and long. The echoes touch every corner of the community.

Four men remain before the courts for the April 5, 1994, robbery-homicide at the Just Desserts restaurant in mid-town Toronto. Lawrence "Brownman" Augustus Brown, twenty-five, is charged with first-degree murder; Oneil Rohan Grant, twenty-two, Emile Mark Jones, twenty-three, and Gary George Francis, twenty-two, each face one count of manslaughter and twelve counts of robbery.

The facts of the case are fairly straightforward. At about eleven o'clock on the night of April 5, 1994, Georgina ViVi Leimonis, an attractive blond twenty-three-year-old part-time telephone operator, was among about thirty people enjoying cake and coffee at the popular restaurant.

Four men entered the restaurant, apparently looking for a table. They left, and about ten minutes later three returned, leaving one outside, presumably in a waiting getaway car.

One man pulled out a double-barreled shotgun and they began robbing the staff, herding the customers to the back wall of the restaurant, taking purses and wallets. Some customers resisted and one was hit with the gun butt. The gunman pointed his shotgun in the general direction of the crowd. It went off, and two shotgun blasts hit Leimonis in the chest.

She fell to the floor, still conscious, as the men fled. Leimonis was still alert when an ambulance took her to St. Michael's Hospital, where she died, hours later, on the operating table.

The murder took the city by the heart. A massive funeral was held at the St. Demetrios Church. There was a huge outpouring of grief from family members, friends and complete strangers. Flowers and candles were left at the Just Desserts restaurant. The senselessness of the murder left newspaper columnists and radio editorialists wondering what Toronto had come to, fearing the encroachment of American-style violence.

Metro police, meanwhile, were quite aware of what Toronto had come to. A massive dragnet was dropped over the city, and the investigators kicked doors across Metro. Several raids failed to turn up the prime suspects in the case, but violent Jamaican posse members were rousted and arrested. One was the brother of one of the city's most notorious gang leaders; another was wanted by the immigration department.

The heat was incredible. On April 14 Lawrence Augustus Brown, "Brownman," went to his lawyer and surrendered to police.

Oneil Rohan Grant was arrested more than a week later. He appeared in Old City Hall courts, smiling for the media and threatening to bite the nose off court officers. Screaming in Jamaican patois, Grant called the guards "bloodclots."

In September, Gary George Francis gave himself up to homicide detectives who, with the Emergency Task Force, raided a downtown apartment. Emile Mark Jones surrendered after detectives found him at a west-side apartment.

The wails of grief over the Leimonis killing became a howl of rage when it was learned that Oneil Grant had already been ordered out of Canada in November 1993. But the Immigration Refugee Board gave him a five-year stay after he pleaded for a second chance. He was required to keep out of trouble until November 1998.

In the midst of the uproar over Grant, Metro Police Constable Todd Baylis was shot dead while patrolling a housing project. The accused in that case, Clinton Gayle, had also been ordered deported to Jamaica but the order was never carried out.

The families of both Leimonis and Baylis hit the federal government with a $111.5 million lawsuit, alleging immigration department officials were negligent in not enforcing deportation orders against Gayle and Grant.

"This action is not about money—it's about accountability and changing the system so that these kinds of tragedies won't happen in the future," said lawyer Tim Danson, acting for both families.

Unlike most homicides that die down relatively quickly for everyone except immediate family and close friends, the Leimonis slaying was still an ache in the chest of the city a year later.

On Sunday, April 2, 1995, another memorial was held at St. Demetrios Greek Orthodox Church. Metro Police Chief David Boothby and the former city mayor June Rowlands were among the two thousand people who filled the church. There remained, among the tears of pain and smiles of remembrance, a strong, enduring anger against the federal government.

And in an epitaph that has become rhetorical, Bishop Sotirios asked the mourners two simple questions: "Is it too much to ask that we all love each other for who we are?...Can't we all live by this principle?"

THE TEENAGE THRILL-KILLERS

THE LAUGHING KILLERS were thirteen, fourteen and fifteen years old.

The bloodied, bludgeoned victims were seventy-five and seventy.

The murders of Rev. Frank Toope and his wife, Jocelyn, sent shock and revulsion through a Montreal suburb in early April 1995.

Montreal police found the bodies of the victims in the blood-spattered bedroom of their bungalow in suburban Beaconsfield. Both had suffered several blows to the head delivered by a base-ball bat. Severe injuries on their hands showed they had tried to protect themselves. The killers took a hundred dollars in cash, a radio and some jewelry.

But, as it turned out, the motive for the grisly slayings was not robbery. One of the three teens arrested "felt like killing some-body," Lieutenant-Detective Claude Lachapelle said.

The youths had been together the night before the savage attack and one of them said he just wanted to commit murder. One of the trio suggested the elderly couple. They had once been customers on his newspaper route.

The couple were attacked at one in the morning on Sunday, April 2. The details of the murders threw the quiet, mainly Anglo community into shock. Frank Toope died from several head wounds. He had injuries to his face, chest, hands and arms. Joce-lyn Toope had been bashed at least half a dozen times in the head and face.

As a team of six homicide detectives worked the crime scene and began an intense investigation, two of the three teens were bragging to their friends about the killings. Disgusted, the friends went to police.

The three were quickly picked up. And police got another shock: two of the suspects, the fourteen-year-old and the fifteen-year-old remained defiant. They laughed and made jokes in the back of the police cruiser as they were transported for booking.

Both gave the finger to reporters and court officials. Police said the youngest of the group seemed in shock.

The community's sadness turned to outrage. The Toopes were well known and liked throughout the area. Frank Toope had, until his retirement in the late 1980s, been rector of St. Mary's Anglican Church, near his home. He and his British-born wife were the parents of a son and daughter. Stephen Toope, thirty-seven, is dean of McGill University's law school. There was a Toope street in the neighborhood.

Neighbors described them as a caring couple, deeply involved in their church and their community.

The case brought more condemnation on the Young Offenders Act, which says the trio face a maximum sentence of three years in a young offenders' facility, followed by two years less a day on parole.

Crown prosecutor Louis Miville-Deschenes is contemplating moving the case into adult court where a conviction would result in a maximum sentence of ten years.

A SICK DOCTOR

Montreal—April 1995

A Quebec judge found a Montreal plastic surgeon charged with raping an anesthetized female patient could not be blamed for succumbing to her.

Dr. Marc Bissonnette, thirty-nine, was acquitted in early April of sexually assaulting a woman he'd treated for four years. On the night of July 6, 1993, the victim had gone to Bissonnette's clinic, where she had had an operation to replace her breast implants. Her mother and aunt testified they arrived to pick her up, they found the door locked. Peering through a partly shaded window into the ground-floor operating room, they saw the doctor exposing his penis, then having sex with the unconscious woman.

Bissonnette was charged with sexual assault.

At the trial, Quebec Court Judge Pierre Brassard rejected the women's testimony, saying they were either mistaken or had made up their statements. He accepted Bissonnette's lawyer's contention that the woman had mistaken a piece of medical equipment for his penis.

Brassard said the doctor couldn't be blamed for succumbing to the woman, noting she'd had sex with a bartender she'd only known for a few months.

Bissonnette was found not guilty.

Brassard's comments enraged women's groups across Canada.

Although he dodged the bullet in the courthouse, Bissonnette was convicted by the Quebec College of Physicians of sexual assault.

END OF THE ROAD

Toronto/Halifax—April 1995

Stolen cars worth more than $1.5 million did a U-turn on their way to Nigeria when Canada Customs and Toronto police forces cracked a massive international theft ring in early April 1995.

Thirty-one vehicles, mostly Jeep Grand Cherokees and Hondas, were stolen from the Toronto area. All were loaded into falsely labeled shipping containers and sent to Halifax by rail. From there, the vehicles were bound for Europe and on to Nigeria.

Police seized the cars and small trucks on the East Coast and in France, Belgium and Nigeria.

Peel Regional Police auto squad detective Jeff Davis said there are a lot more cars in the hot-wheels underground and many will be recovered.

It's the second major seizure of stolen cars bound for Africa. In November police rounded up $1 million worth of various vehicles, also bound for Nigeria.

Police believe the stolen-car rings are part of a global organized crime network, and they think the problem is growing.

A Jeep is worth more than twice its North American value on the Nigerian market.

Also in April, Montreal police busted a similar ring shipping stolen vehicles to Haiti. Residents alerted police when they saw cars being loaded into large containers at an east end industrial park. Four men were arrested and five vehicles were seized.

BANKS SCOLDED

Winnipeg—April 1995

If banks won't protect themselves from fraud, a judge asked, why should he?

Winnipeg judge Frank Allen came down hard on banks during a trial in April 1995.

Allen was conducting the trial of a man accused of using a bank machine to deposit three two-hundred-dollar cheques into an account containing only twenty dollars. Each time the man put in a two-hundred-dollar cheque, he withdrew the same amount. But the cheque were returned because the account had insufficient funds.

The man pleaded guilty to fraud and was given a conditional discharge. He was ordered to repay the money.

Allen said bank machines make it easy for fraudsters: "I have talked to people in the banking industry about what I think of these machines...they ask for this kind of trouble."

CRIMINAL HARASSMENT

Scarborough—Apirl 1995

Three days after she married Wain Schmidt, Sharon Perreault was on her way to becoming a battered wife, and her new husband was on his way to prison.

Schmidt, forty-six, of Scarborough, Ontario, was convicted of the relatively new charge of criminal harassment on April 6, 1995, after a jury was told of a wave of terror and physical and mental abuse aimed at Perreault.

The court was told that the campaign of abuse began three days after the couple were married and continued until they separated six months later. But Schmidt followed his estranged wife, entering her house without consent and ominously warning her to "check her brakes."

Mr. Justice George Ferguson called Schmidt "a man of violence with an uncontrollable temper and absolutely no respect for women." He said the former bouncer, who has thirteen criminal convictions, including assault against his wife, was on two probation orders requiring him to stay away from her. He also had thirty-four convictions for property and forgery offenses.

When Crown attorney Anna Maleszyk suggested a prison term of three and a half years, Schmidt called out: "I might as well have killed her." Justice Ferguson sentenced Schmidt to two and a half years in prison.

But Perreault said she remains in fear of her life: "I really believe he's going to come back…and do something worse."

POISON IN THE FORMULA

Toronto—April 1995

Toronto detectives arrested a west end man April 8, 1995, after an eight-month-old baby boy had his formula spiked with kitchen cleanser.

Staff-Sergeant Dan Marshall said Old Dutch Cleanser was found in the infant's powdered formula. The child's baby-sitter was mixing formula when she noticed the color was off. When she mixed another batch and the same thing happened, she took the formula to a clinic and the cleanser was discovered.

The baby wasn't injured.

Romwel Bello Prado, twenty-nine, was charged with attempted murder and other crimes. Police said the suspect knew the baby's mother, adding, "It was a jealousy thing."

A MOTHER'S ANGUISH

An anguished mother cried, "It's not enough, it's not enough," as her eight-month-old daughter's father was sentenced to four years in prison for permanently disabling the child.

Francisco Santana, twenty-two, of Metro Toronto, was accused in the May 1994 assault on his daughter, little Vanessa Chaulk.

The court was told that Santana, who was alone with the child, dropped Vanessa four feet, then violently shook her in what was described as a "moment of madness, anger or rage."

Vanessa suffered severe life-threatening injuries. Ambulance personnel were taking her to the Hospital for Sick Children, but on the way changed their route to another facility where she underwent brain surgery that saved her life.

Prosecutor Donna Armstrong said: "Vanessa will never live a normal life.…The force used to cause these injuries was unimaginable…" She asked for a five-year sentence, noting Vanessa will never be able to be physically active and will suffer speech disabilities.

As Santana cried in the prisoner's box, Justice Victor Paisley called him "grossly immature" and urged psychological counseling.

The four-year sentence wasn't acceptable to Patricia Chaulk, Vanessa's mother. She said Santana should "win an Oscar for his crying performance," adding: "She's my miracle baby…she wasn't supposed to live."

WELCOME TO CANADA?

A Jamaican-born criminal with twenty break-and-enter convictions won't be booted out of Canada because he's been here since he was eleven years old.

Patrick Alexander McKenzie, thirty-one, was granted a three-day stay by the Immigration and Refugee Board in early April.

The board heard that McKenzie came to Canada in 1975 and began collecting criminal charges in 1980. In November 1994 he was released on probation from a two-year sentence for breaking into the same liquor store twice.

But his lawyer argued McKenzie came to Canada when he was eleven years old and shouldn't be deported to a country he doesn't know.

A WILD CANADIAN WEEKEND

Cross Canada—April 1995

Civilization slipped its leash during the second weekend of April when a tremor of gun violence shuddered across the country.

The crime wave sparked new life to the volatile gun-law controversy, with Justice Minister Allan Rock's gun registration system getting a boost of fear and support. Antiregistration forces said it was unreasonable to believe the proposed gun laws would have prevented the rash of incidents.

Canadian Press reported firearms-related incidents that included:

- The death of a Winnipeg teen who was hit by a blast from a sawed-off shotgun while he and his friends were examining it;
- The wounding of a policeman in Amherst, Nova Scotia, as he tried to arrest a man at the town's police station;
- The hostage-taking of a twelve-year-old boy during a running gun battle after a department store holdup;
- The shooting of a deaf sixteen-year-old male during a card game in Burnaby, British Columbia.

THE PURPLE CLUE

Haileybury—April 1995

A theft probe in a Northern Ontario town came to a quick end when a twelve-year-old boy showed up with purple hands and a purple face.

Ontario Provincial Police were investigating thefts of cash at a school in Haileybury in mid-April when they decided to dust a ten-dollar bill with a powder that turns purple when it comes in contact with water. The bill was left in a teacher's coat pocket, and it quickly disappeared.

A short time later a student with purple dye on his hands and face was spotted. He was confronted by teachers and police. OPP said punishment would be left up to the school.

MAN STALKS ELEVEN-YEAR-OLD

London—April 1995

A thirty-seven-year-old man who found an eleven-year-old girl "good-looking, sexy and voluptuous" pleaded guilty to stalking her.

Garth Thompson of London, Ontario, was remanded into custody April 5 pending a probation investigation.

Prosecutor Heather Carpenter told the court Thompson met the girl in June 1994 and began sending her expensive gifts and love letters. One card described the preteen as "good-looking, sexy and voluptuous." A typed letter read: "I love you now and will always love you and nothing [her parents] can say will ever change that."

He also sent a registered letter containing poems and a twenty-dollar bill, Carpenter told the court. Later he sent a three-hundred-dollar portable stereo and several other gifts, addressing them to the "vivacious" and "absolutely gorgeous" girl.

Thompson, who lives within a block of the victim's home, was repeatedly warned to stay away.

Lawyer Mike Barry said his client is "an academic eccentric" who posed no threat to the child. The university-educated Thompson, who has a degree in physics, was a "dysfunctional oddball," Barry told the court.

MOTHER OF TEN KILLED IN RANDOM SHOOTING

Edmonton—April 1995

A double murder in north Edmonton on April 7 brought renewed cries for major adjustments to the Young Offenders Act in a case that left a taxi driver and a mother of ten children dead.

Trevor O'Dell, sixty-two, was hit in the head by bullets seconds before two fifteen-year-olds jumped from his still-moving taxi. The cab went out of control with the gravely wounded driver still behind the wheel. The vehicle sped through a stop sign and crashed into a car driven by Alexia Lema, fifty-eight. Lema, a grandmother with ten children, was killed. O'Dell was pronounced dead a short time later.

Two teens were spotted running from the scene.

The following Monday two fifteen-year-olds were arrested and charged with two counts of murder and weapons offenses.

Both appeared in youth court and were remanded in custody.

Police said robbery wasn't a motive for the O'Dell shooting.

The suspects' court appearance came one year after another shooting involving Edmonton teens. In that case Scott Farion, seventeen, died of a gunshot wound to the head as he and two passengers in his car passed around a stolen pistol. The gun discharged, killing Farion. A sixteen-year-old male was convicted of manslaughter in that case and sentenced to two and a half years in youth jail.

Farion's mother, Joyce, was in the courtroom as the O'Dell–Lema suspects appeared. She said she intended to follow the current case: "Kids are getting away with murder," she told the *Edmonton Sun*. "They look at the two and a half years [Scott's killer] got and they see there are really no consequences. I feel driven to see that that's changed."

Alberta Justice Minister Brian Evans was moved to call for the death penalty for juveniles with a history of repeated violent crime. "I have been on record as saying that in limited circumstances I think there's a place for the death penalty—that is where there is a consistent pattern of total abuse of the normal rules and regulations of society," Canadian Press reported Evans saying.

He added that prosecutors are considering trying to get the case moved to adult court. Alberta has lobbied Ottawa to put some teeth into the Young Offenders Act.

FOR THE LOVE OF MOM

Edmonton—April 1995

An Edmonton, Alberta, man committed "an act of love" in the mercy killing of his elderly suffering mother, an Alberta provincial court ruled April 7, 1995.

Robert Cashin, forty-six, had pleaded guilty to administering a noxious substance. A charge of attempted murder was stayed.

Alberta provincial court Assistant Chief Judge Peter Caffaro learned that Murielle Cashin, sixty-eight, was suffering from cancer when Robert sat on her bed in October 1994 and gave her an overdose of medication.

Cashin said he'd promised his mother when she was diagnosed with breast cancer two years earlier that he wouldn't let her suffer. As his mother's condition deteriorated, Cashin lived with her, cooked for and fed her, and accompanied her to her daily radiation treatments.

On the night of October 18, 1994, he gave her the overdose. She died three days later in hospital, not as a direct result of the overdose but from the family's decision to take her off life support. When she died she weighed barely sixty-five pounds.

Judge Caffaro gave Robert Cashin a suspended sentence and two years' probation. He said to jail Cashin would be "contrary to the whole philosophy of criminal law."

Outside court, Cashin told reporters, "You don't think of the laws when this happens. When you have somebody in so much pain, the laws become irrelevant."

MARGARINE SEX ASSAULT

Halton Hills—April 1995

A sixty-two-year-old man was sent to prison for a year after a six-year-old girl was smeared with margarine and sexually assaulted.

Piere Van Grootel, of Halton Hills, west of Metro Toronto, was sentenced April 11 after pleading guilty to sexual assault. The court was told the victim's family had trusted Van Grootel and allowed him to take three young children for an overnight visit at his home.

During the visit the six-year-old was smeared with margarine and molested. The six-year-old told another young girl what happened, and the second girl got to a phone and called her parents, who immediately took her to the local Ontario Provincial Police detachment.

Van Grootel's lawyer, David Harris, told Mr. Justice James Carnwath his client had put the margarine on the girl to relieve an itch.

In addition to his jail time, Van Grootel was sentenced to three years' probation and ordered to stay away from any female under the age of sixteen unless an adult is present.

THAT LONG DISTANCE FEELING

Hamilton–Wentworth—April 1995

A major police project in Hamilton–Wentworth began with a single telephone call and ended with the arrests of several people—including the sons of a murdered Mafia boss—and the seizure of $20 million worth of cocaine.

Project One-Call began in 1994 and targeted Domenic and Giuseppe Violi, both of Bunkerhill Drive in Hamilton. Detectives said the Violis are related to Giacomo Luppino, the elder statesman of the Calabrian Mafia in Canada.

U.S. Drug Enforcement Administration agents worked with the Ontario Provincial Police, the RCMP and Hamilton-Wentworth detectives to crack the case, which led to the region's largest cocaine haul.

Police said the cocaine, seized in Joplin, Missouri, had originated with the Colombian cartel and was destined for the Canadian drug ring.

In early April police rounded up nine suspects from Quebec, Metro Toronto and Hamilton. All face drug charges and several are charged in an arson fire set at a Guelph-area restaurant in 1994.

Detectives said the ring is indicative of the new north-south drug organizations involving Colombian gangs and Italian criminals in Canada.

CHILD-PORN RING CRACKED

Toronto—April 1995

Earlier in his life John Herbert Young, fifty-seven, collected stamps.

But when police raided his downtown Toronto apartment in 1993 looking for child pornography, they found he'd switched from stamps to sex tapes. And a lot of the tapes were child pornography.

Young, described as Canada's "kingpin of kiddie porn," was

the biggest dealer police had ever dealt with, Judge John Hamilton said. "You had a library of films and your place looked like a Jumbo Video store."

Young and a group of associates were targeted by Project P, a joint OPP-Metro Police investigation into the selling of explicit kiddie porn. When the police raided Young's apartment, they found thirty-nine hundred tapes, of which a hundred and fifty were child pornography. Fifteen of the videos used local Toronto kids aged ten to seventeen.

Staff-Sergeant Bob Matthews of the OPP led the probe. He said a couple of the local teens who participated in the making of the videos had attempted suicide.

On April 18, 1995, Young pleaded guilty to possession and sale of child pornography. Judge Hamilton sent Young to prison for two years: "People have to get the message the courts will impose penitentiary terms even for first offenders," he told the convicted man. "Your group of friends are small in number but active and none of you seem to understand the harm you do...the damage to children."

Two days after Young's sentencing, the Project P squad raided another downtown apartment. Matthews said magazines, pictures and drugs were seized. "Some of the children in the photos are prepubescent," he noted.

ONE BODY TOO MANY

Ste-Marie-De-Beauce—April 1995

On Thursday night, April 27, 1995, undertaker Clement Mercier took a step toward death when he embalmed a lifelong friend in the Quebec town of Ste-Marie-De-Beauce.

"Everybody knew Mercier would lose it whenever he embalmed a friend," a neighbor told the Canadian Press. "He just couldn't take it. He would drink for days and go through dark, very angry periods."

The April 27 embalming ended in double murder and suicide. After processing his friend's body, Mercier went home to his neat two-story yellow brick home and got into an argument with his common-law wife, Celine Faucher. Early Friday morning Faucher left her home and went to a neighbor's house where she called police. Mercier's ten-year-old daughter, Cindy, remained inside. Faucher tried to get back inside to get Cindy, but Mercier refused her admittance.

At seven o'clock, police chief Denis Nadeau responded to the call to the Mercier home, unarmed. He'd been there before for similar calls and had known the embalmer for fifteen years.

Nadeau arrived at the scene in his unmarked car and parked in the driveway. He stepped out of his car and saw Mercier in front of the home.

"Come and see what I did to my daughter," Mercier yelled at Nadeau, before opening fire with a shotgun. Nadeau was hit twice, once in the head. He fell mortally wounded beside his car in front of the house. For three hours he lay beyond help as police set up a command post and sealed off the residence. An armored car was brought in from Quebec City and, hiding behind it, police were able to remove his body.

Unaware that Cindy had been killed, was already three hours dead by the time Nadeau was gunned down, police tried to negotiate with Mercier. At two o'clock Friday afternoon they recorded the last sign of life inside the home.

At four-thirty Saturday morning, police managed to approach the home. They saw Cindy lying dead between the living and dining room areas. She had been hit by three shotgun blasts fired through a cupboard door where she'd tried to hide from Mercier.

Fearing Mercier was lying in wait, police used the armored vehicle to smash in the home's windows. There was no sign of activity inside. At one in the afternoon they crept in and found Mercier hanging in a stairwell, one end of a nylon clothesline tied around his neck, the other tied to a banister.

A SHOCKING CRIME; A DRUNKEN DEFENSE

Montreal—April 1995

A seventy-three-year-old man who successfully used drunkenness as a defense for dragging a woman from her wheelchair and raping her won't face a second trial.

A Quebec Court judge ruled on April 27, 1995, that Henri

Daviault can't receive a fair trial because new victim testimony is unavailable. The testimony is unavailable because the handicapped woman died.

Daviault was charged in the May 1989 attack in which the victim was wheeled into her bedroom, dragged from her chair, thrown on the bed and raped.

At his trial, Daviault, a chronic alcoholic, testified he couldn't remember anything about the incident, except that he woke up naked in the woman's bed. He said he'd consumed more than half a dozen beers and most of a forty-ounce bottle of brandy before the attack. He was convicted at his first trial and sentenced to a year in jail. But he appealed the case to the Supreme Court, arguing he was too drunk to know what he was doing. In September 1994 the court ruled that extreme drunkenness could be used as a defense. A new trial was ordered. But the victim of the rape had died in 1992, and Judge Gerard Girouard ruled it would be a violation of natural justice and the Charter of Rights and Freedoms to simply read the victim's testimony from the first trial into the record. The Crown offered no evidence, and Daviault was acquitted.

TEEN PACK MURDER

Dawson Creek—April 1995

Six teenagers face murder charges after a drifter was found beaten to death and dumped by the side of a road in Dawson Creek.

James Alex Baldwin, fifty-eight, had arrived in Dawson Creek about three weeks before he was murdered on April 19, 1995. Described as a man who was "down on his luck," Baldwin had refused to accept welfare and was living in a tent while he looked for work.

Police said his body was found by a city worker on April 20. He had been savagely beaten about the head. On April 28 detectives arrested six male youths, ranging in age from fifteen to seventeen. All were charged with second-degree murder.

No motive for the killing was revealed.

An officer described the victim as "kind of a proud guy."

A TEXTBOOK ROBBERY

Ottawa—April 1995

As an emergency call it scored an A in getting a policeman's pulse racing: a report of a bank robbery in progress, and three suspects wearing nylon masks, clutching guns in their hands.

As a school project it rated a hard F.

But at least no one died.

Police in Ottawa raced to a Bank of Nova Scotia on Bank Street on April 25, 1995, after a passerby spotted two people in masks, armed with pistols, going inside.

Sergeant Ken Doyle, the first officer at the scene, looked inside and saw a person with a gun. He called for backup and seven officers sped to the scene. Three suspects were ordered out; one came outside clutching a gun but the three were arrested without incident.

After interviewing the youths, police found they were part of a video drama course. They were playacting with the cooperation of the bank manager, who hadn't notified police.

A plastic gun and a video were seized.

Sergeant Doyle said things could have turned out very differently: "One of them came out of the bank with a gun in his hand and had he turned on an officer, [the officer] may have had to react....There could have been very serious injuries in this."

DAD ACQUITTED OF SPANKING DAUGHTER

London—April 1995

An Illinois man, charged with assault after publicly spanking his five-year-old daughter during a trip to London, Ontario, was acquitted in late April after a two-day trial.

David Peterson, his wife, Paula, and their two children, Rachel and two-year-old William, were on a visit over Labor Day weekend in 1994 when a passerby saw Peterson spanking his daughter in a restaurant parking lot.

The passerby called police and Peterson was arrested and spent a night in jail before being released.

At the trial, Judge John Menzies was told Peterson, thirty-nine, spanked his daughter as a disciplinary measure after she pushed William out of the family car and slammed the door on his fingers as he tried to get back inside. Peterson said he'd warned Rachel not to close the door but she did it anyway. He said she got a "bare-bottom spanking" because she tried to kick him when he went to swat her covered bottom.

The court was told the Petersons were responsible parents who seldom resort to physical punishment. Most disagreements were solved through discussion and withholding of privileges.

After Peterson's acquittal, he told reporters that the interest in his case was "a legitimate one."

"A large public debate just landed on us," he said. "We stepped in it."

GRIMSBY CAR THIEF

Grimsby—April 1995

Police in Grimsby, Ontario, made a no-brainer arrest when a car thief broke into their surveillance van in late April.

Constables Jim Prinsen and Les Vuyk were operating the car-theft stakeout in the Beamer Conservation area. They were keeping an eye on a decoy vehicle in a parking lot when a man drove up. He pulled on a pair of gloves and strolled over to the decoy vehicle.

First the bandit tried to break in through a locked window, then he realized the front door was open. He jumped in, and Prinsen and Vuyk jumped up.

A Hamilton man—described by an officer as "sold without batteries"—was charged with attempted theft.

Canadian Press

Marilyn Tan

THE TITILLATING TRIAL OF MARILYN TAN

IT WAS A case only the 1990s could produce. A tale of glamour and glitz, of high finance, high jinks and the high life.

And of AIDS and sex and death.

The woman at the center of the scandal was Marilyn Tan, a thirty-five-year-old former model, who by all accounts was much desired by men in the higher social circles of Edmonton.

Tan, a Filipina-Canadian, photographed beautifully and had a dark, mysterious aura.

But in 1995 she faced a charge of aggravated assault for injecting a former lover with AIDS-infected blood during a bout of sadomasochistic sex.

The Alberta passion play began in the 1980s when Tan and man-about-town society photographer Con Boland started a torrid affair.

Tan, young and gorgeous, had had a rough start to her life in Canada. The youngest of eight children born into a poor family in Manila, she came to Canada in 1977, settling first in Winnipeg. She married a Filipino-Canadian and they moved to Saskatoon, where she gave birth to a son. The couple separated less than a year later. In 1982 Tan moved to Edmonton and applied for welfare. She worked odd jobs, one of them as a singer in a club where her dark exotic looks attracted more interest than her voice. Two years later she spotted a help-wanted ad describing the job of assistant to Con Boland.

Boland, a famous Dutch-born photographer with a taste for drugs and sex, lived an upscale life that took him into the cream of society. His prosperous photo studio catered to high-scale clients, among them prime ministers, premiers and members of the city's business elite.

The couple hit it off immediately, and an intense relationship ensued. But the relationship gradually went into a tailspin. The romance that began with the couple singing to each other and lunching together almost daily dissolved by 1991 into continuous arguments and recriminations. Tan came to believe she'd been used by Boland, that she'd been instrumental in building his photo business and that she deserved half of the firm. And she thought he was seeing other women, that the bloom was coming off his rose because she was getting into her thirties.

The situation went from bad to worse. In December 1992, Rachel Deitch, a friend of the couple's, told Boland he might have AIDS. Boland told her she was "being silly."

Things remained static for six months until Tan left Canada to visit her family in the Philippines. Then, carrying a box Tan had entrusted to her, Deitch again went to Boland. The box contained evidence that Tan had been offered $2 million to be the mistress of a wealthy man. It also contained details about another man who had bought her a mansion and leased her a $60,000 automobile.

In December 1992 Boland tested positive for HIV. Earlier the same year he'd tested negative.

On July 16, 1993, Tan was arrested on charges of aggravated assault, conspiring to administer a noxious substance and administering a noxious substance. She was also charged with uttering death threats. (Three other men, millionaire Geoffrey Clarkson, one of Tan's lovers, and two private security men, were charged in connection with an earlier acid attack on Boland. The trio's charges were stayed by prosecutors, who said they had insufficient evidence to proceed against the men. Boland has lasting scars on his chest and neck from the acid attack.)

At her trial, which began in May 1994, the Crown alleged that Tan had twice injected Boland with tainted blood, once at his home in April 1992 and again three months later during a wild bout of sadomasochistic sex after he was lured to a Holiday Inn in Long Beach for "a last-time farewell." During the farewell, Boland passed out after sex, he said, and when he awoke there was a bruise on his leg. The Crown alleged he had been injected with AIDS-infected blood supplied by Tan's sister, Evelyn, a registered nurse in the United States.

Crown prosecutor Brian Peterson said Tan wanted revenge on Boland for breaking off their seven-year relationship. He said, "All she could think about was revenge." Peterson said Tan also talked about shampooing Boland's head with hair remover.

Peterson petitioned for anonymity for the "Fairy Godfather," a prominent Edmonton businessman who would be testifying in the case. He asked that the Fairy Godfather be allowed to testify from behind a screen because publication of his name could harm his family and business. He said the mystery man—one of Tan's lovers—was expected to testify he offered Tan $2 million if she agreed to be his mistress.

Court of Queen's Bench Justice Keith Ritter took a pass on that one, agreeing to hear arguments later in the trial.

The court also heard details of a death threat. The victim of the threat was Boland's girlfriend, Jeanette Kunkel. Kunkel, twenty-nine, said she'd fallen in love with Boland in 1992 and that he told her he had split up with Tan a few months earlier. Once when Kunkel phoned Boland, Tan answered the phone and said she and Boland were making love. She invited Kunkel over to watch. The death threat came when Tan—"sinister looking" and decked out in black leather and stiletto heels—visited Kunkel at work in June 1992 and threw her up against a wall. Tan, Kunkel said, told her to break off her relationship with Boland or she'd have her killed by gangsters.

Kunkel believed Tan wasn't fooling around. Within hours she'd jumped on a plane to Vancouver. "I was scared for my life," she testified.

Con Boland testified about his lengthy relationship with Tan. He said things got rough during the 1991 recession, when Tan continued to spend money at a rate that put him $20,000 in debt. Even though things were on the skids in 1992, Tan, her mother, a sister and Tan's fifteen-year-old son continued to live in Boland's house while he lived across the street.

When the Tan moved out in October, she began seeing multimillionaire Geoffrey Clarkson, former dean of business at North-eastern University in Boston. Clarkson sent Tan on a trip home to the Philippines, and the next day Boland was served with a statement of claim from his ex-lover.

A short time later mutual friend Deitch approached him and told him about the plot to infect him with HIV. She handed over the box of documents. Boland got an HIV test, which came back positive. He took the documents to police. Among the documents was a love letter from the mysterious Fairy Godfather to Tan, offering her $2 million to become his lover for ten years.

Boland said he went to the Fairy Godfather, a former business client, for help finding Tan after Deitch approached him. He said the man originally denied any involvement with Tan but eventually offered to help in the case if his love letters and photographs were returned.

Boland told the court of the night of rough sex with Tan in California. He said, "She had promised some really wild love making." He said Tan was a whip-wielding dominatrix and he acted as the servant, blindfolded and wearing only a jockstrap and clips on his nipples.

He was given a few drinks from a bottle supplied by Tan's sister, who had taken an adjoining room. He fell into a deep sleep after just a half a glass of liquor, he said. When he awoke he found a large bruise on the back of his upper left thigh and a pair of smaller bruises on his right thigh. Tan told him he'd hurt himself on the way to the bathroom the previous night.

Boland testified that after the California treat Tan refused to kiss him or have sex, but, he noted, they sometimes masturbated each other.

Boland detailed the circumstances of his own sex life, saying he'd first hired a prostitute at the age of nineteen and continued using prostitutes throughout his life. He said he always wore a condom with prostitutes but admitted he didn't use condoms with some girlfriends. He also told the court he had never had a homosexual relationship. He said he sometimes pressed a vibrator against his anus to arouse himself. He also said he liked dripping hot wax from a candle onto his nipples. And, among his sex toys, he described a leather device that snapped around his testicles.

He said he had used a wide variety of drugs, ranging from heroin and cocaine to marijuana and hashish. He said he had injected some drugs, but that he never shared a needle.

After several days of testimony, Justice Ritter ruled that the mystery man in the case, the Fairy Godfather, also known as Mr. Smith, wouldn't be permitted to testify anonymously. He said Bruce Sansom, an Edmonton millionaire, "has made life-style choices" and can't hide from the results of those choices.

Sansom, fifty-nine, was the chairman and owner of Managed Investments Ltd., an investment firm for pension funds. The firm handles more than $500 million in assets. Married for thirty-six years, he has four grown children.

Justice Ritter said Sansom's business continued to be successful even though many of his social and business circle were aware of his affair with Tan.

Meanwhile, Rachel Deitch, Tan's former best friend, took the stand and testified she helped concoct the plot to inject Boland. Deitch said she revealed the plan because she was afraid of being killed by Tan's sister.

She said she and Tan and Tan's sister Evelyn conspired to shoot HIV-infected blood into Boland. She said Evelyn sent the blood to Deitch's home. Deitch admitted receiving the blood and giving it and some syringes to Tan. But, she said, "I never believed that any of this could come to pass...never." She said Tan told her about the injections after the California trip. "I never believed that a friend of mine would actually do it. I always believed her love for him would outweigh her anger." Deitch said she tried to get people to believe her story about the plot, but when no one did, she took the box of Tan's private documents to Boland and warned him.

Deitch, forty-nine, said she wore a hidden tape recorder during a meeting with Tan in an attempt to get evidence about the plot.

Bruce Sansom, refused the anonymity he sought, was forced to detail in open court his relationship with Tan. He said he'd met Tan and Boland in July 1991 when he went to have a portrait done at the studio. He became friends with both of them and, he said, tried to repair their deteriorating relationship. By April 1992 he had become involved with Tan. He said they met a couple of times a week and fell in love. He gave her a bracelet and a watch and cash. He said Tan broke up with him to take up with Geoffrey Clarkson. Clarkson, he said, bought Tan a diamond ring and diamond earrings. He also leased a luxury car for her.

Sansom testified about his lunch meeting with Boland. Sansom said Boland was furious that Tan had launched a lawsuit in a bid to get a share of the portrait studio. He said Boland swore he'd go to the media with the letters from Tan's private box unless Sansom agreed to persuade Tan to abandon her lawsuit.

Outside the court, Sansom said the alleged $2 million payoff for a ten-year affair was merely an investment opportunity. He described himself as a victim in the case. He said he was "a bit of a player....I'm not even involved in this thing." He said he'd made amends with his family.

Alberta's top infectious-diseases expert testified that Boland was a regular patient at the provincial sexually-transmitted diseases clinic. Dr. Barbara Romanowski said the photographer had been treated several times between 1977 and 1984 for gonorrhea and chlamydia. Tests done after he contracted HIV in 1992 showed he also was infected with hepatitis B. As well, the court heard, in February 1994, a year after he tested HIV-positive, he sought medical treatment for herpes sores on his buttocks.

In the end, after eleven days of testimony that ranged from pathetic to amusing, the judge acquitted Tan of all charges except threatening death. Tan wept with joy as the three most serious charges were dropped. But when she was sentenced to three months in the slammer for threatening, she lost her smile.

Justice Ritter said he simply couldn't believe Boland when he testified he couldn't have become HIV positive other than through Tan's alleged injections. Reviewing Boland's sexual history and his bent for sadomasochistic sex, the judge said he believed it was out of character for Boland not to have had several sexual relationships with prostitutes in 1992, the year he was infected. "I simply cannot believe Mr. Boland lived near celibacy in the 1992 calendar year," he commented, noting that Boland's history of sexually transmitted diseases disproved his claim that he was a practitioner of safe sex.

After the trial, Boland told reporters he was "disappointed" in the outcome of the trial, but said he still loved Tan. "I have never not cared for her....She's a good woman. She just got off track and became vengeful."

Tan was whisked off to the Fort Saskatchewan jail, where she was put to work peeling potatoes for inmate meals. The glamorous dominatrix, used to soft beds and the finest bedding, spent her first night sleeping on a thin mattress on the cement floor.

EIGHTY-TWO-YEAR-OLD FIGHTS BACK

Palmerston—May 1995

At age eighty-two, Oscar Noll was hardly the Charles Bronson of Palmerston, a town of some three thousand people north of Guelph, Ontario.

But when he fired on two young thugs who broke into his shop at three o'clock on the morning of January 18, 1995, he became a local celebrity.

A local celebrity facing assault charges.

The feisty jeweler was working late when the men burst into his store. Noll dove to the floor, crawled to a counter where he kept a small .32-caliber pistol hidden, and opened fire, missing both suspects. They fled the shop and were later arrested, charged and jailed for burglary.

Police charged Noll with possessing a firearm and with assault.

Local residents widely supported Noll, holding fund raisers, a garage sale and a dance, and signing petitions on his behalf. The last Saturday in April was declared Oscar Noll Day by the town council.

In May the Crown withdrew the charges and Noll was granted a conditional discharge by Judge Casimer Herold and ordered not to possess a firearm for one year.

"He struck a chord with the silent majority...which believes that you have a right to protect your life," lawyer Calvin Martin said.

BASKETBALL ROOKIE-OF-THE-YEAR CHARGED WITH BRUTAL BEATING DEATH

Regina—May 1995

When Pamela Jean George, a twenty-eight-year-old mother of two, was found dumped near a ditch by the side of the road three kilometers from Regina, she became Saskatchewan's first homicide of 1995.

The details of the murder were shocking enough. Police determined she'd been picked up by two men and driven out of town, where she had been attacked. An autopsy on the bloody and battered body of the native Canadian woman showed she had been sexually attacked and beaten to death.

Regina RCMP had little to go on, and they appealed to the public for help through the Crime Stoppers program. It wasn't until the end of the first week of May that investigators received a tip that focused the probe on a pair of suspects.

When the arrests came, the shock of the George slaying was eclipsed by the details of the men picked up by the RCMP.

First to drop was Steven Kummerfield, eighteen, a University of Regina education student. The popular basketball star had been named the Great Plains Athletic Conference 1994–95 rookie of the year. He was arrested at his father's home in University Park, an upper-middle-class neighborhood. Kummerfield's car was seized.

After a brief court appearance on May 10 he was remanded into custody until May 17.

James Hills, head coach of the U of R Cougars men's basketball team, told Kevin Blevins of the *Regina Leader-Post* he was in "total shock" at the arrest. "The worst thing you expect to hear from a player is that he failed a class," he said. "But you never expect anything like this."

Detectives said they were looking for a second suspect who

had left the province. They said they expected an arrest in the next few days.

And when it came, the arrest was as shocking as the first. RCMP picked up nineteen-year-old Alex Ternowetsky. Ternowetsky was arrested near Fort St. James, a British Columbia logging town a hundred kilometers northwest of Prince George.

Ternowetsky's father had taught social work at the University of Regina and was currently the chairman of the social work department at the University of Northern British Columbia in Prince George.

On May 22, after a five-hour hearing, both teens were denied bail and ordered held in custody at the Regina Correctional Centre. Court of Queen's Bench Justice Gene Maurice told them not to speak with each other and not to communicate with Crown witnesses.

SILENT BANDIT

Toronto—May 1995

One of the country's most mysterious bandits, a man who never spoke a word and who pleaded guilty by nodding his head, was sent to prison for seven years in May 1995.

Known only as John Doe, the suspect was arrested on November 8, 1993, after the brazen robbery of a bank shipment in east Toronto.

The silent suspect and two other men armed with assault rifles robbed a Brinks truck of $200,000 in a daring daylight heist. A Brinks guard, Carlos Sousa, was slugged with a rifle butt, momentarily knocking him out. Sousa recovered his wits and chased the bandits, watching them jump into a getaway car. Sousa opened fire but missed the men.

Police spotted the car later and arrested one man. No money was recovered.

Throughout questioning and booking, the man, apparently from Eastern Europe, refused to utter a sound. When he wanted a lawyer, he showed a note to a guard, then apparently ate it.

Metro Police holdup squad detectives attempted to trace a

bulletproof vest the mute miscreant was wearing when he was arrested. They found it had been bought in New York City. His clothing yielded no clues: the tags had been removed.

In sentencing Doe, Provincial Court Judge Paul Pickett asked if he had anything to say. Doe shook his head.

"Mr. Doe, I'll be as brief as you are.... You're sentenced to seven years," Pickett said.

RCMP SMASH HEROIN RING

Vancouver—May 1995

An international heroin smuggling network was smashed by RCMP drug officers in 1995.

The seizure was called the largest in Canada. Street value of the ninety-percent-pure smack was in the hundreds of millions of dollars. RCMP Staff-Sergeant Tom Brown said the heroin, labeled Double Uniglobe Brand, was seized over the last weekend in May. It was hidden in hollowed-out wooden packing crates.

The shipment was tracked from Bangkok to Seattle, Washington, where some of the drugs were removed. The remainder was allowed to continue through Vancouver to Toronto as part of a "controlled delivery." Police raided two homes in Scarborough. Four Asian men face several drug-related offenses.

Brown said Metro Toronto plays an important role as a transshipment point for heroin.

Andrew Vaughan/Canadian Press

Lorelei and Steven Turner

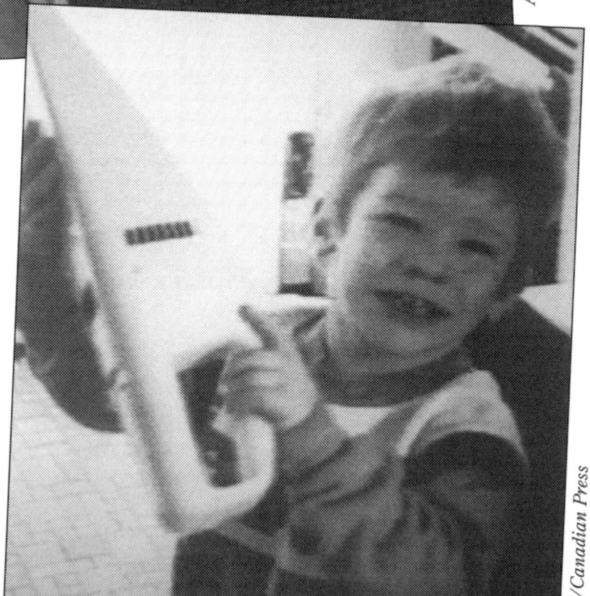

CBC/Canadian Press

John Ryan Turner

THE HEARTBREAKING, SHORT LIFE OF JOHN RYAN TURNER

AT THE END of May 1994 military police were called to the immaculately kept home of Corporal Steven Turner and his wife, Lorelei, on Canadian Forces Base Chatham, on the Miramichi in New Brunswick.

And they were confronted by a horrible sight.

John Ryan Turner, the couple's three-and-a-half-year-old son, was unconscious. He weighed just under twenty-one pounds, about half the weight of what an average child his age should weigh. He had broken bones. His genitals were burned bright red by urine trapped in his unchanged diaper. His penis was bleeding and his hip bones and rib cage were sticking out. There were abrasions on his body that appeared to be caused by being confined in a steel-studded leather harness. A harness with rivets and metal clasps was later found in the boy's bedroom closet.

Police seized a saliva-stained sock, believed to have been used as a gag.

The child's hair looked like straw and his body was so shrunken that his head appeared huge. His eyes jutted out of his face, and his skin was stretched over his cheekbones. There were sores on his mouth.

Johnny Turner was taken to hospital where he was officially pronounced dead, but it was a formality. An ambulance attendant who transported him said he was cold to the touch and very gray in color, a condition, he said, that indicated the boy had been dead for a while. A pathologist found John died of starvation and apparently hadn't eaten in four weeks.

On his arm was a bite mark, gnawed by eight tiny teeth, a V-shaped wound, apparently self-inflicted.

Within hours of the discovery, police arrested the Turner parents on manslaughter charges.

The parents' trial, before a judge only, began a year to the day after the body was found. In his opening statement prosecutor Fred Ferguson told the court he would show "a background of physical abuse and neglect."

He said the victim suffered from "psychosocio dwarfism," an environmentally induced psychiatric abnormality he also described as the "failure-to-bond disease." The condition, Ferguson said, was caused by lack of bonding between a mother and child. It can cause weight loss and deterioration of the body.

"The failure to thrive is the heart and soul of this matter," he added, noting that the child, even at his young age, had two missing teeth and had suffered three or four broken bones in his short life.

Barry Whynot, who represented Steven Turner, indicated the direction his defense would take. "In this case, you're going to see a number of government agencies which are going to have to explain their conduct—community services, mental health, some of the doctors involved. There are a number of issues that are going to come out."

A month before he was found dead, John Ryan Turner, slightly more than three and a half years old, was at the rear of the Turner home, struggling to get up the back stairs. "Mommy, I in house?"

Lorelei Turner yelled at him: "Get your belly off your knees, that's why you're always falling....If you can't get up the steps, you'll stay out."

He was bent over, trying to pull his foot up a step. He was shaking and shivering, and neighbor Jeff Mallory, who like many area residents thought the child was recovering from an illness, softly urged him: "Come on, Johnny, you can do it."

When Lorelei didn't move to help the boy, Mallory couldn't watch anymore: he turned away.

Another neighbor remembered seeing Johnny sitting alone and ignored in the yard for nine hours on a cold early spring day.

A family friend was so upset by the boy's grayish skin and bald spots on his head that she dialed her own doctor three times to get assistance. But each time she hung up. That was three weeks before he died.

Valerie Zimmer described Johnny Turner's deteriorating appearance: "He looked like an old man in a little boy's body. He looked trapped. I wanted to go over and hug him but I couldn't. I just kept staring."

Zimmer said she suffered nightmares after the boy was found dead. She said she blamed herself for not taking action, saying she believed Lorelei Turner when she said the family had consulted a doctor. In fact, the family hadn't seen a doctor for more than eighteen months.

In May, after Zimmer and her parents hadn't seen Johnny playing on the family's new swing set in the yard, they became even more concerned about the boy. They decided if they didn't see him by the end of the week, they'd call the child welfare authorities.

But it was too little, too late. On Thursday morning, Steve Turner came over to use their phone to call an ambulance. He said he thought his son was dead.

The Turners had two children. Johnny was firstborn, followed by Amanda in 1993.

Two months after Johnny was born, Lorelei Turner called the province's public health service. She told the public health nurse she couldn't cope with her baby crying. "Do I have to do something to my baby to get somebody to help?"

Nurse Cynthia Hillier said Lorelei was depressed and not prepared to be a mother.

In August 1992, when he was two, Johnny was taken to a pediatrician who noted that Lorelei's "anger and frustration centers on John Turner far beyond what is expected."

A student at a ceramics class with Lorelei said she notified the Child Protection Agency in 1993 that there was a large bump on Johnny's head. Apparently no action was taken.

Testimony at the wrenchingly emotional trial painted a family landscape of blackness and heavy gray, with little or no light.

John Anderson, head of the child-protection team at the Izaak

Walton Killam Hospital in Halifax, and David Meek, a pediatric neurologist, told the court they believe Johnny Turner was rejected by his mother from the moment he was born. When Amanda was born in 1993, the boy's diminished status in the family led to a deep depression. The depression probably resulted in Johnny refusing to eat. In turn, the malnourishment led to a downward-spiraling medical condition that went untreated.

Anderson described the child lying alone in a darkened room, bound by the harness, a sock jammed so tightly into his mouth that the skin became cut on the edges of his mouth. The sock, he said, was used so the parents wouldn't hear him crying.

Evoking a scene of rejection and loneliness, Anderson populated it with Johnny in his dark room with the blinds drawn as the parents had a party outside, playing on a new swing set with their one-year-old daughter, Amanda.

Lorelei Turner, he said, had suffered sexual abuse when she was a child, and her father committed suicide when she was in her late teens. He said she sank into a deep depression. When Johnny was born, she ignored him and, he said, she frequently swore at him.

Steven Turner, described as a well-built macho man, had cared for his son when he was a baby, but in late 1993 decided to ignore him so Lorelei and Johnny could make a stronger bond. Although Steven Turner wanted to separate from his wife, he didn't leave and spent most of his time fishing with his friends.

Neurologist David Meek summed up nature's solution to the world Johnny Ryan was born into: "If his world was impossible to live with or live in, then nature took over and said, We cannot survive, we'll stop eating and waste away."

His voice sometimes cracking during his highly emotional summation, Crown Prosecutor Fred Ferguson said Steven and Lorelei Turner caused John Ryan Turner's death. He said the parents committed manslaughter because they failed to provide the necessities of life for the child.

"No parent sits around and does nothing about the life of a

child," he said, noting Lorelei often belittled the child and refused to touch him. "It's hardly imaginable that a father living in the same home...would consider there was no problems with this emaciated child."

He said strong evidence showed Johnny Turner had been physically abused in the months before his death. Both arms had been broken, apparently as a result of being violently hit. "If you find that these people gagged this child in the face of this kind of emaciation...that takes away any chance of reason or common sense prevailing." He said the reason the parents didn't get medical help for Johnny was that they feared the physical abuse would be detected.

The Turners' lawyers, who offered no evidence in the case, said the Crown failed to prove that the parents caused Johnny to starve to death.

Barry Whynot, Steve Turner's lawyer, said Johnny wasted away and that the physical injuries weren't the cause of death. He said that while the Crown had implied Johnny was bound and gagged as he starved to death, there was no evidence to show that was how he died. "Mr. and Mrs. Turner were as confused about what was going on as everyone else."

He added, "The Crown hasn't proven that they withheld food from their son. What was withheld was emotional support and that's different. Is that a necessity of life? There would be an awful lot of parents indicted on that charge."

Lorelei Turner's lawyer, Brian Doucet, said the death was "completely unexpected." He told the court the parents were suffering from a shared mental illness.

Doucet told reporters that the Turners alone can't be blamed in the case, "It's apparent on the evidence that all these people, whether they were professionals or lay people, if they had simply taken the opportunity to get involved, to blow the whistle, to raise the red flag, that there would have been an early intervention and John Turner wouldn't have suffered this tragic fate."

On Wednesday, June 15, Mr. Justice Riordan found the Turners guilty of killing their son.

Outside the courtroom a crowd of about two hundred people cheered and called abuse; motorists on the streets honked their horns.

"Hang 'em," some spectators called, while others yelled, "Murderers."

The Turners cried as they were led away in handcuffs. They had the dubious distinction of being the first parents in Canada to be found guilty of manslaughter for failing to provide the necessities of life to their child.

Inside the packed courtroom, Justice Riordan said it was hard to understand what went wrong: "It's not possible…to make any sense of what happened."

Justice Riordan described Johnny Turner as "a severely ill boy" and noted: "John Ryan Turner was a powerless young child who was totally dependent on the care of his parents. He did not receive the care that he needed and was expected.…His short life was extremely sad, his death, tragic."

A month after being convicted, the couple returned to court for sentencing. Calling the death of John Turner "deplorable," Judge Riordan sentenced the parents to sixteen years in prison.

THE HOUSE HERMIT'S REIGN OF TERROR

Vancouver/Toronto—June 1995

A former antique dealer, dubbed the House Hermit, who conducted a reign of terror against women in Vancouver in 1992 was sentenced to six years in prison for kidnapping in early June 1995.

David Alexander Snow, forty, was already serving an indefinite term as a dangerous offender after several Vancouver women were sexually attacked during the summer of 1992. Snow was arrested after a massive police dragnet in North Vancouver.

At the time of the Vancouver attacks Snow was under investigation in Toronto for several offenses, including the kidnapping of one couple and the double murder of another man and woman.

The victims in the double homicide were real estate agent Ian Blackburn, fifty-four, and his wife, Nancy, forty-nine. The two were found by relatives in their car, which was parked in the driveway of their upscale Toronto home. Police believe the Blackburns were kidnapped at their farm home northwest of Toronto and driven to their city home.

Snow won't be tried for the Blackburn murders until 1997.

But in early June 1995 he was convicted of kidnapping Sam and Rose Appleton from their Georgian Bay cottage, north of Toronto.

The Appletons went to their cottage in March 1992 and were confronted by Snow, who had been living in the building for six weeks. The Appletons were forced to drive Snow to Toronto, where they were robbed of cash.

Snow pleaded guilty and was given six years for kidnapping, break and enter, robbery and use of a firearm.

SWALLOW

Toronto—June 1995

A Toronto drug dealer was convicted after a woman who swallowed a four-thousand-dollar piece of rock cocaine choked to death.

Dexter "Dread" Browne, twenty-three, "wanted Audrey Greiner to vomit the crack so he could sell it," Madam Justice Marie Corbett said, noting he showed "wanton and reckless disregard" for her life.

Greiner, nineteen, died in April 1994, four hours after swallowing a half ounce of cocaine in a baggie so a raiding party of police officers wouldn't seize it. Dread Browne told another woman he'd take the victim to hospital but waited until she was almost dead.

Browne was convicted in late April 1995 of criminal negligence causing death. On June 9 he was sent to prison for four years.

"Even criminals can have duties toward one another," Madame Justice Marie Corbett said, adding that Browne "appears to live in a complete moral vacuum."

STAR ATHLETES CONVICTED OF GAY BEATING

Two star athletes scored six months in jail after they were convicted of an unprovoked attack on two gay men in Toronto, Ontario.

And while Justice Nicholson McRae didn't go so far as to call the vicious assault a gay bashing, he said that "hate played a role in the incident."

The victims were walking in the downtown area when they were confronted by Vincent Iacozza, twenty-one, of Stoney Creek, and David Cvetan, twenty, of Hamilton. The victims testified they had to jump from the path of a speeding car the two assailants were riding in. One man in the car asked, "What are you looking at?"

One victim said, "Nothing."

Both men jumped from the car and punched one victim and put the boots to the other. During the attack the accused men yelled, "Fucking fags," and, "Fags."

While Justice McRae wasn't convinced the assault was a hate crime, Crown counsel Michael Leshner said similar incidents are a serious problem in Toronto and that gay men and lesbians are increasingly at risk.

Bernie Farber, of the Canadian Jewish Congress agreed: "Physical attacks are mostly targeted against the gay and black community, and they seem to be increasing."

Both the Crown and the convicted men's lawyers plan appeals.

BAD TIMES: BIGGER GUNS

Two weeks after Ottawa police constables Leslie Maley and Jim Pietrkiewicz were shot during a bank stickup, the city police services board okayed the purchase of a thousand Glock semiautomatic pistols.

Maley and Pietrkiewicz cornered three men after a holdup on March 23, 1995. Both officers were shot by the suspects. Neither suffered life-threatening wounds.

Increased violence against the public and law enforcement officers has led to an increasing number of agencies using firearms that hold up to sixteen bullets.

THE COST OF CANADIAN JUSTICE

StatsCan reported $9.6 billion was spent in 1992–93 on the Canadian justice system, up from $7.2 billion in 1988–89.

Most of the 1992–93 budget went for policing, a jump of slightly more than 30% from the previous five years.

Legal aid added up to $603 million, double what it had been five years earlier. Court spending rose 35.6% to $867 million. Correctional services for youths, including administration of the parole board and incarceration, tallied $488 million; adult services added up to $1.9 billion.